General editor: Graham Handley MA PhD

Brodie's Notes on Daniel Defoe's

A Journal of the Plague Year

Graham Handley MA PhD
Formerly Principal Lecturer and Head of English Department, All Saints College, Tottenham

Pan Books London and Sydney

First Published 1988 by Pan Books Ltd
Cavaye Place, London SW10 9PG
9 8 7 6 5 4 3 2 1
© Pan Books Ltd 1988
ISBN 0 330 50241 7
Photoset by Rowland Phototypesetting Ltd
Bury St Edmunds, Suffolk
Printed and bound in Great Britain by
Richard Clay Ltd, Bungay, Suffolk

This book is sold subject to the condition that it
shall not, by way of trade or otherwise, be lent, re-sold,
hired out or otherwise circulated without the publisher's prior
consent in any form of binding or cover other than that in which
it is published and without a similar condition including this
condition being imposed on the subsequent purchaser

Contents

Preface by the general editor 5

Daniel Defoe: life, background, works 7

The Great Plague 12

Fact and fiction 14

Summaries, critical commentaries, textual notes and revision questions 16

Defoe's narrative art in *A Journal of the Plague Year*

The narrator 48

Incidents 55

Style 57

Religion 60

General questions 62

Further reading 64

At the time of writing, there is only one readily available edition of *A Journal of the Plague Year* in print. This is The Penguin English Library Edition of the work, with an Introduction by Anthony Burgess, together with his clinical summary of the Plague. There is a note on the text by Christopher Bristow, and the occasional editorial comment or definition at the foot of the page in the text.

References in this Brodie's Note are to the Penguin edition (first published in 1966), but since this commentary follows the straightforward narrative it can be used with any edition of the text.

Preface

The intention throughout this study aid is to stimulate and guide, to encourage the reader's *involvement* in the text, to develop disciplined critical responses and a sure understanding of the main details in the chosen text.

Brodie's Notes provide a summary of the plot of the play or novel followed by act, scene or chapter summaries, each of which will have an accompanying critical commentary designed to underline the most important literary and factual details. Textual notes will be explanatory or critical (sometimes both), defining what is difficult or obscure on the one hand, or stressing points of character, style or plot on the other. Revision questions will be set on each act or group of chapters to test the student's careful application to the text of the prescribed book.

The second section of each of these study aids will consist of a critical examination of the author's art. This will cover such major elements as characterization, style, structure, setting, theme(s) or any other aspect of the book which the editor considers needs close study. The paramount aim is to send the student back to the text. Each study aid will include a series of general questions which require a detailed knowledge of the set book; the first of these questions will have notes by the editor of what *might* be included in a written answer. A short list of books considered useful as background reading for the student will be provided at the end.

Graham Handley

London in the 17th Century — with some outlying areas mentioned in DEFOE'S account (Penguin edition p. 167)

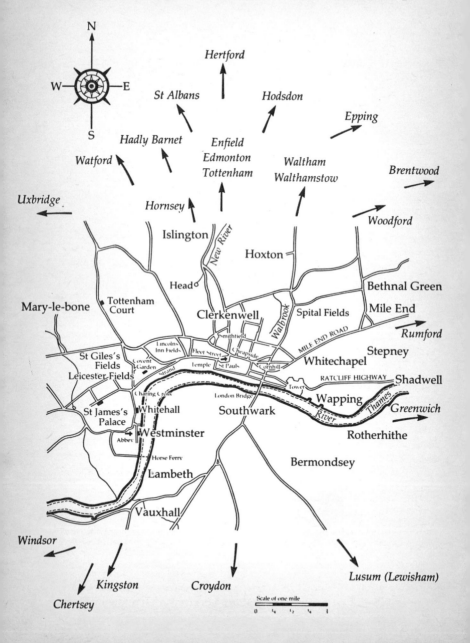

Daniel Defoe: life, background, works

Daniel Defoe was almost certainly born towards the end of 1660 in Cripplegate, London, the son of a tallow-chandler, his original name being Foe. The year 1660 witnessed the end of the Commonwealth and the restoration of the monarchy in the person of Charles II. Defoe was of Puritan stock and thus a Dissenter, for the Restoration ostensibly restored the Church of England to its proper place – though in fact this period was marked by a decline in religion and a widespread upsurge of licentious and dissipated behaviour, particularly prevalent in the young men about town and some of the aristocracy.

As a small boy Defoe was in London for two of the most momentous occurrences in the history of that city, namely the Plague and the Great Fire. The first is the subject of this study, its form being rather that of a supposed documentary than fiction. Early in 1665 the first signs of the plague began to appear in St-Giles-in-the-Fields. By May it had spread into other parishes; the suffering was extreme and panic had set in. The King and the Court left London, the rich went where they chose, the poor often remained and died, the law-courts ceased to function. Infected homes and shops were shut up on the orders of the magistrates, and people who remained walked down the middle of the streets rather than risk the contagion from the houses on either side. Though Defoe may not have been in London for the whole of the Plague, there is little doubt that his apparently eye-witness account derives in part from memory and perhaps even more from other older eye-witnesses who impressed the various terrors on the mind of the imaginative child. *A Journal of the Plague Year* is significantly factual in its tone and emphasis, and we are not surprised to discover that there was a saddler called Henry Foe living in Aldgate at this time. He was probably Daniel's uncle, and the nephew may have got the information he retails with such superbly simulated authenticity from his uncle's diary. It seems likely that Defoe's family were strict Dissenters. He has recorded that he himself set to copying out the Bible in shorthand in case the Roman Catholics became powerful and persecuted them (the Dissenters), since Charles II's brother James was a Catholic.

In that little world in which he lived, the Dissenters had been hit first by the Act of Uniformity (1662) and then the Conventicle Act two years later which heaped restrictions upon them. Following hard upon this unease came the Plague, followed by the Great Fire of London which broke out in September 1666. It ravaged the city, though James Foe's house was one of those which survived. His son has recorded that he never forgot the terrible spectacle which he 'saw with a sad heart'.

Defoe shows in his writing the ability to judge clearly what is right and wrong, though in life as he grew older he was not able to act always with a strict sense of morality. Certain things he undoubtedly inherited from his early years – he had, for instance, a Puritan's dislike of the theatre. He was well-read though, for example in the verse of his great Puritan contemporary John Milton, who published *Paradise Lost* in 1667.

Defoe was educated at an academy in Newington Green which was quite enlightened for its time, concentrating on modern languages, such as French and Italian, and science rather than the classics. There he picked up a broad education and tasted a variety of subjects. By 1680 he had determined to become a merchant, and thereafter we find him travelling much in pursuit of his commercial concerns in Europe. He was a great one for travel in England too, invariably going on horseback. He married in 1684, and in the following year was dangerously involved in the Duke of Monmouth's rebellion (he later said he was 'in arms under the Duke of Monmouth'). To quote from his biographer James Sutherland (see *Further Reading*), he was 'a born adventurer'. Soon he was greeting the accession of William and Mary (the Protestant succession now assured), but he began to incur increasing losses through speculation. He also seems to have had an unwise and fatal fascination for the law, and there is evidence of a number of instances in which he was either the defendant or the plaintiff. He was taken to court in the early 1690s, and in 1692 he was bankrupted with debts of £17,000, an immense sum of money in those days. He apparently went into hiding (almost certainly in Bristol), but he seems to have placated his creditors. By 1705 he had considerably reduced his debt. It was in that year that he became a government agent, though his actual movements and responsibilities are obscure. In the closing years of the century he had owned a brickmaking plant. Meanwhile, his family increased (two boys and six girls) and it is possible that he had an illegitimate son as well.

Gradually Defoe became known as an author, particularly of political pamphlets, initially attacking the isolation of Tory policy from European commitments. His poem *The True-born Englishman* stresses the polyglot nature of our racial characteristics. This poem made him a reputation and put him on very good terms with the King and his Whig government. (The Tories were the conservative party, the Whigs were akin to our Liberal party.) But in 1701 the Tories came to power. Various representations were made to the House of Commons to counteract the threat of the French. Defoe was unwise enough – and brave enough – to present *Legion's Memorial* to the House ('the Englishmen are no more to be slaves to Parliaments than to a King. Our name is LEGION, and we are many . . .'). Through writing like this Defoe was the voice of the Whigs in opposition, but with the death of the King Defoe's position was changed. The High Church faction had come to power, and one of their avowed policies was to proscribe the activities of the Dissenters. Defoe carried their potential practice to a kind of parody in his cunning pamphlet, *The Shortest Way with the Dissenters* (1703), where he ironically suggested that Dissenters should be banished and their preachers hanged. At first misunderstood as being supportive of their aims, it provoked the Tories to decisive reaction, and it also upset some of Defoe's fellow-dissenters. A warrant was issued for his arrest, an informer gave away his hiding-place, and he was condemned to stand in the pillory. Much as Defoe dreaded this, the popular tide was flowing in his direction, and flowers rather than stale vegetables or bricks greeted his appearance. He even wrote a *Hymn to the Pillory*, which is really a plea for a wider justice than he had been shown. In a sense, though, through popular recognition and acclaim he got it.

He now began to work for the Tory Secretary of State, Robert Harley, who secured his release from Newgate Prison in return for the contributions of his pen. He became a Tory journalist, writing for Harley's periodical the *Review* a series of articles and attacks, the latter making him many enemies. His own bankruptcy made him vulnerable to attacks in return. Within a year or so he had become an agent in the pay of Harley, travelling much and discovering what he could about the political views of important citizens in the country at large. He reported, for example, on the situation in Edinburgh prior to the Act of Union between England and Scotland in 1707. With the discrediting of Harley and his resignation over treasonable irregularities, Defoe was temporarily in trouble but, after a request to Harley, he was employed by another Tory Minister, Godolphin. But following the trial of Sacheverell, Godolphin himself lost his position. After Harley had been restored, Defoe's articles in the *Review* aroused hostility from the Whig opposition. Harley also began to employ Dean Swift (the author of *Gulliver's Travels*) as a pamphleteer, and there was a steady drift towards High Tory policies which was repugnant to Defoe. Once more he was arrested, this time for some outspoken pamphlets on the succession to the throne (either the Pretender or the House of Hanover when Anne's death should occur).

However, he was pardoned by the Queen. She died in 1713, and by 1715 the Whigs were in potent power, Harley and Bolingbroke having been impeached and disgraced. Again Defoe was before the courts, this time for a libel on the Earl of Anglesey. After his release, with characteristic opportunism and dexterity, Defoe transferred his allegiance once again to the Whigs and began to work for them.

This is followed by the most extraordinary turn of all. Now nearly sixty Defoe, satirist, pamphleteer, religious and political controversialist, occasional poet (and no mean writer of verse) began to write fiction. *Robinson Crusoe* was born.

Defoe, vastly experienced in life and in intrigue, but lacking the usually required basis of a privileged education, found a new reading public with his first major work of fiction, which was issued in 1719. *Robinson Crusoe* was reprinted many times in Defoe's lifetime, perhaps largely because its hero was from the lower middle classes and had a general appeal. Defoe now continued to write prolifically, though not always with success, that is, the commercial success for which he strove throughout his life. In 1722, in addition to *A Journal of the Plague Year*, he published *Due Preparations for the Plague*, *Moll Flanders* and *Colonel Jack*. *Roxana* appeared in 1724. These are the works, together with *Robinson Crusoe*, for which he is chiefly remembered. James Sutherland (see p.64) has summarized Defoe's fictional concerns admirably:

The world's goods fascinated Defoe, and in his fiction he was able to stroke and handle imaginatively those commodities that as a merchant he had once actually dealt in.

His fictions are both worldly and moralistic, almost mirror images of the man. If we take Moll (in *Moll Flanders*) as an example, we find that the self-confessed tart has a heart; her honesty, her admissions and her susceptibilities make her narrative an endearing one despite our moral judgments of her. *A Journal of the Plague Year* will be examined in some detail in the course of this commentary, but what it has in common with his other fiction, I am inclined to say with all his writing, is the author's engagement with and reflection of life. He and his characters share the same zest for life as their experiences record. Even when Defoe is being moralistic, we suspect that he both admires and reproves his wayward characters like Roxana. He has an acute if somewhat unsophisticated psychological insight, direct and uncompromising in its revelation of human motives. He often focusses on one character and enters completely into that character's motives and experiences. This is what gives his portrayals such an unerring veracity.

For the last part of his life he continued to engage in business, to write books and produce journalistic work. Apart from his *Tour Through the Whole Island of Great Britain* (1724–7) he also wrote *A History of the Devil* (1726) and an *Essay on the History and Reality of Apparitions* (1727). He died in 1731. Sutherland has, I think, correctly indicated his major qualities as a writer. He calls his prose:

> A workmanlike, unpretentious, admirably familiar form of expression, which puts the reader at his ease without passing into the over-colloquial, it is the prose of democracy ... A page of Defoe – almost any page – is still astonishingly alive.

It is the right note of appraisal. And in *A Journal of the Plague Year* that life breathes vibrantly in the terrible surround of death.

The Great Plague

The reader of *A Journal* will see how close Defoe keeps to the facts of the plague. The first signs were 'two Risings about the bigness of a Nytmeg' on each of the sufferer's thighs. Apparently Dr Hodges (the Dr Heath of *A Journal*) had a patient who exhibited these tokens about Christmas 1664. In the succeeding months official figures of deaths from the plague were put at just below 70,000, but Defoe is probably right when he puts the total at about 100,000 or more. He hints at the fact that because other reasons for death were given in the bills of mortality, people's fears were diminished. Another point which Defoe makes and which was certainly a fact is the onset of and continuation of the severe winter from November until March, during which period there was little sign of the devastating spread to come. According to Lord Clarendon, who had the other earlier plagues in mind, by April 1665 the richer families were leaving the city. Permission was given for the building of more hospitals (Defoe refers to them as pesthouses), Parliament was dismissed (to be possibly recalled in September).

The plague spread rapidly in May and June (just as in Defoe's account). Houses which were infected were marked with a red cross, the air was supposedly rid of infection by the burning of fires, the doctors worked overtime and alcohol was considered to be a useful antidote to the infection. All these things are mentioned in Defoe's account. The dead-carts were often driven by servants whose employers had departed, and there was much robbing and looting. Since graveyards soon became filled, the smell of death and corruption was ever-present. Soon the authorities adjusted to the position by ordering the digging of large holes or pits with quicklime added in to them. But at the height of the plague many of the dead could not be buried immediately and were stacked in the streets. Trade was at a standstill, dogs and cats were slaughtered, and quacks made a fortune – or died. These things are stressed by Defoe. The King went to Hampton Court. By August, the death-roll was up to 2,000 per week. The Lord Mayor and his magistrates effectively ran the city. Houses were shut up for forty days if one of the inmates had plague, watchmen were employed to guard them, but the inmates frequently escaped. Lodgers were forbidden in the city, the streets were often putrescent with the corpses of rotting animals, and the dead-carts were often seen, their drivers crying 'Bring out your dead!'

Outside in the country, towns and villages alerted by news of the plague barred their doors – or defended their walls – against fleeing Londoners. Letters posted to country districts were disinfected by steam or water before being opened. Those citizens of London who decided to leave the shore and live on boats often survived the plague, a point taken up by Defoe in his account.

With the height of the Plague in the City in September a number of people went mad and acted in a distracted manner, some bringing about their own deaths. The peak was in the third week of September, when it is thought that between 12,000 and 14,000 died, though the official figures were well below this. Thereafter there was a decline. By Christmas things were returning to normality, and in February the King returned to London, soon followed by the wealthier citizens who had taken care of themselves. Ironically, another devastating tragedy was only a few months away.

In their superb *London Encyclopedia* Ben Weinreb and Christopher Hibbert note that the nursery rhyme 'Ring-a-ring o'roses/A pocketful of posies' is really a memento of the Plague. The first line refers to the colour and shape of the signs of the disease, the round tokens which signalled its onset and its fatality. The sneezing which now seems so innocent was apparently a common indication that death was upon the sneezer.

Fact and fiction

This section would usually be headed *Summary of the Plot*, but such is Defoe's craftsmanship that I have decided to call this brief appraisal *Fact and Fiction* for two self-evident reasons: firstly, the Plague was fact, and secondly, Defoe's account of it through a supposedly autobiographical narrator is fiction. Defoe, as we have seen, was interested in calamities in particular (matched perhaps by his obsession with the occult and the nature of providence), and there is little doubt that he drew on published sources in his account of the Plague and its spread. These he combined, with rare felicity of judgment, with anecdotes and stories he had heard as a child, into an arresting and frightening fictional whole. The result is a triumph of art, so much so that it conveys a solidity of realism. As Sutherland has indicated, 'the very circumstances with which he is dealing impose a certain order on his narrative . . . the first weeks of anxiety when the infection is spreading, then the appalling period when the Plague is at its height, and finally the weeks of gradual improvement when life returns to the grass-grown streets and the rumble of wheels is heard once more on the cobbles.' The supposedly autobiographical mode suited Defoe (witness *Robinson Crusoe*) and, as Louis Bredvold has observed (in his *The Literature of the Restoration and the Eighteenth Century*), '*A Journal* is ostensibly a diary of the year 1665 kept, without any thought of publication, by a London saddler.' He too pays tribute to the fact that 'Such an illusion of actuality is really a triumph of the creative imagination', adding that 'once Defoe is admitted to the category of novelist, he must be ranked as one of the great realists'.

No attempt has been made in the following commentary to locate Defoe's sources: we are concerned here with the evaluation of fiction which derives from an established fact. Historians differ about the effects and even the intensity of that fact, though to the city dwellers of the time it must have seemed to be (followed as it was by the Great Fire) a divine visitation, retribution, holocaust. G. M. Trevelyan takes the view that it hardly affected 'the onward movement of the power, opulence and population of the capital'. He traces the successive manifestations of the plague (noting the 30,000 deaths from it at about the time of the succession of James I, a similar number dying when Charles I came to the throne), and sees the outbreak of 1665 as striking 'the imagination more, for it came in an age of greater civilisation, comfort and security'. Sir George Clark, on the other hand, points out that the bills of mortality at its peak registered some seven thousand deaths in a week. After noting that the suffering and the panic were constantly recurred to in the writing of the time, he tells us that 'The methods used for coping with it were either futile superstitions, or measures that made it actually worse.' There is no doubt that Defoe's account would testify to the latter.

The reader of this commentary should first study Anthony Burgess's admirably succinct clinical summary of the Plague in the Penguin edition, and then read *A Journal*, noting the various physical manifestations indicated by Defoe. It would be an error of emphasis to suggest that *A Journal* can be read purely for enjoyment, but such is Defoe's narrative art that a certain pleasure does come into it despite the gruesome nature of the subject matter. Often Defoe is concerned with presenting his main character or characters in adversity. *A Journal* is no exception, and the human mix of greed, opportunism, fortitude and courage is presented with a telling realism of the highest order – the effect when imaginative truth and felt detail encompass the reader in all their urgency.

Summaries, critical commentaries, textual notes and revision questions

It is important to remember that *A Journal of the Plague Year* is not divided into chapters but is one continuous narrative sequence. Accordingly, for the purposes of this study, page references to the Penguin edition are here given so that the student may conveniently note the main aspects of Defoe's narration, his narrative art and any significant critical or factual references as he or she reads. This is an arbitrary way of dividing the text, but hopefully it will bring the student to a detailed understanding of it.

1 up to p.29, '. . . but in the imagination, especially at first'

The main area covered here is from September 1664 onwards, with the increase in the mortality bills from December 20 to February 14 (1665). There is a brief reference to the 'preceding visitation of 1656' (p.26). There is a general dying down in the cold winter but an increase in the number of cases towards the end of April 1665. This accelerates in May, the narrator observing that the authorities distorted the truth somewhat by not saying that most of the deaths which occurred were as a result of the Plague. He records the continuing increase in June, and provides a supposedly eye-witness account of the evacuation of many of the well-to-do people. There are rumours abroad that barriers will be set up on the road to prevent the free movement of people (who may be carrying the plague) and there is a general feeling of panic.

Commentary

The first thing to note is that Defoe sets off with facts, thus deliberately making the reader accept the supposedly authentic viewpoint of his narrator. At the beginning of the second paragraph we find a piece of ironic observation – 'We had no such things as printed newspapers in those days to spread rumours and reports of things, and to improve them by the invention of men.' This is strikingly modern in its appraisal. The note that the government knew about what was happening but kept quiet about it reminds us that Defoe was a government agent from time to time during his career. The style is direct and simple. The lay-out of the facts has the genuine documentary flavour. The eye-witness account is matter of fact, so much so that we should not dream of questioning it. But the narrator builds up an atmosphere of fear, and he also comments ironically on the cover-up which meant that a number of deaths from plague were not included in the weekly totals. This was obviously done in the hope of quieting people's fears, and Defoe shows his awareness of this psychological approach from those in authority who have most to fear from a public outbreak. The spread in June and the ensuing panic is done with narrative verve, the pace of the prose keeping up with the temperature of the populace crowding, for example, the Lord Mayor's door. Already we are made aware of the narrator's compassion for what he sees.

private Secret.
Long Acre... The main places mentioned in London throughout this commentary will be found in the map on p.6.
gotten some vent... Was much talked about by people locally.
the Hall Guildhall, from where the administration of London under the Lord Mayor was undertaken.
weekly bill of mortality List of deaths (in the particular parish).
distemper Illness, here the plague.
easy Made comfortable in our minds.
possessed the heads of the people They were obsessed by the idea.
moderate i.e. in number.
the preceding visitation of 1656 According to G. M. Trevelyan (*English Social History*) the last major outbreak was in 1636, but since the 17th century was plagued with plagues, Defoe obviously has a specific instance in mind.
spotted-fever Typhus.
liberties Districts subject to control by the municipal authorities.
knavery and collusion Dishonesty and conspiracy.
articles i.e. entries.
without Outside.
turnpikes Gates with collectors who exacted a toll from road-users.

2 up to p.35 '... or with myself on that subject'

The move here is from the general to the particular, the author's own case. His main concern is whether to flee the plague or not. He is a saddler, unmarried, and wonders whether to leave his shop and servants and go with his brother into the country. He has faith in God and believes in divine Providence. He reasons on the matter within himself, and tells his brother that he has decided to stay. But the brother nearly persuades him to change his mind. Again he goes home, ponders, feels himself at God's mercy, and idly opens the Bible at the 91st Psalm – 'Surely he shall deliver thee from the snare of the fowler, and from the noisome pestilence.' This determines him, though next day he is taken ill, thinks initially that it is the plague, and then recovers.

Commentary

The tension of this section is dependent on the inward debate of the author and the nature of his faith. The tone is intimate, confiding in the reader and, despite the fact that we know that he stays (otherwise there would be no book), we are riveted by the debate – the divide between practical selfishness and an abiding faith which accepts what Providence has in store for him. This disclaimer of being a single man is more than balanced by the reference to 'a family of servants' which conveys the warmth of the narrator and his interest in people, an interest which is to be reflected time and time again in the course of the narrative. Yet strangely his decision is affected by chance – his servant, who he intended to take, leaves him and there are other occurrences which make him delay. These he ascribes to Providence, the cornerstone of his faith. Simply put, he accepts them all as 'an intimation from Heaven' (p.32) that he should stay. Notice that the brother is used to ridicule 'predestinating notions' (p.33). The intense nature of his religion is seen in the long quotation from the Psalm which acts almost as a directive from God that he should stay in London. We notice that the paragraph which follows the quotation is a strongly personal expression of faith in God's will. The irony of the illness which is *not* the plague effectively humanises the narrator – this is just the kind of thing that does happen after an important decision.

of moment Important.
farthing A coin of very small value.
in which was embarked all my effects In which everything I had was invested.
the best preparation for the plague was to run away from it Note the direct simplicity of the style which reflects the projected action.
strait Extreme position.
in the war which had not been many years past Since the second war against the Dutch was being fought at this time, the reference must be to the English revolution, which began in 1640 and led to the Protectorate being established under Oliver Cromwell.
always crossed Prevented.
complexly, as they regard one another i.e. to judge events as they happen in relation to other events.
take my lot Take my chance, risk what happens.
take post Hire a horse from an inn on the road.

predestinating notions Fatalistic views.
the bills i.e. of mortality.
the visible call ... my calling i.e. the divine influence ... a sense of duty and responsibility.
This lay close to me The narrator is referring to the Bible.
fowler One who traps wild birds.
noisome pestilence Noxious plague.
my times The period of my life.
meet Right.
out of order Ill.
fetched a round Took a direction.

3 up to p.40 '... there was any (women especially) left behind'

The time is now mid-July, and the narrator encompasses some detail in his account of the eastward spread of the Plague. It waxed particularly fierce in the districts of the poor, for example Clerkenwell and Cripplegate. He goes about the streets as usual, and keeps an eye on his brother's house. By July/August most have fled the city itself, while the King and the Court had already left in June. Of the people in the city who are left the narrator says 'sorrow and sadness sat upon every face' (p.37). In Holborn he finds that people walk only in the middle of the street. The Inns of Court are shut up, and there are few lawyers about in the Temple, Lincoln's Inn or Gray's Inn. At this stage, apart from the wealthy, most people stayed in the Liberties, Southwark, Wapping, Ratcliff etc. He points out that at the end of the civil war and after the Restoration the city and suburbs of London were full, and discourses upon the flourishing commerce and trade of London before the Plague.

Commentary

Again the facts in terms of numbers are mixed in with the account. The narrator shows (a) a certain bravery in walking out about his business and (b) a sense of responsibility over his brother's house. He also appears to be naturally inquisitive. The irony, a kind of radical attitude, is seen in his comment that with regard to the Court 'it pleased God to preserve them' though he cannot refrain from adding that he feels the dissolute behaviour of the Court has brought down the wrath of God on the nation. This is typical of the Puritanical Defoe. The paragraph which succeeds this is a graphic account of the changed face – and the changed faces – of London. It is imbued with the narrator's compassion – 'the shrieks of women and children at the windows and doors of their houses'. The contrast between the present and the past, enjoyment at the Restoration and its aftermath, is vividly brought out.

kept Remained.
levities and debaucheries i.e. giving themselves up to licentious enjoyment and loose, promiscuous living.
to be visited To feel the effects of the plague.
crying vices Their manifest sins (a reference to the licentiousness of Charles II's court).
watchmen Defoe makes clear later that these men were set to guard infected houses, to see that no one left. Their position was often abused – bribes and theft were open to them, for example.
dependences Responsibilities.
intermitted Eased up for a time.
visitation The onset of the Plague.
the wars being over . . . The Commonwealth being overthrown and Charles II being restored to the Crown of England in 1660.
luxurious Voluptuous, given to pleasure.
Akeldama (Aceldama) After the death of Judas, the money he received for betraying Christ was used to buy the Potter's Field as a burial place for foreigners, called 'Blood Acre'.

4 up to p.48 'And the like of men-servants'

The narrator goes back in time once more, mentioning the appearance of the comet several months before the Plague (there was also one before the onset of the fire in the following year). He considers that they are portents of God's wrath, judgement on the city, but then proceeds to an exposure of the variety of quacks who take advantage of such manifestations. At this time they battened upon the credulity of a frightened people through prophecies, interpretations and so on which only succeeded in keeping alive the fear. This abuse sometimes succeeded in driving people mad, and many of the interpretations merely seemed to confirm the idea of God's vengeance. The narrator gives instances of people thinking that they saw things, hallucinations which, once suggested, set up a kind of communal hysteria. As a cautious, even cynical, observer the narrator realizes that others see him as an outsider. There are supposedly ghosts, astrologers preach the 'conjunctions' of planets (p.48), and books are published which serve further to frighten the people. There was some woeful preaching from the Ministers of religion, but despite this the previous divisions were temporarily healed in the crisis by Dissenters being allowed to preach in churches where 'the incumbents were fled away' (p.47). Quacks pretending to tell fortunes plied a busy trade, those practising magic, the black art, even displaying signs outside their doors advertising their spurious capabilities. The 'middling people and the working labouring poor' (p.48) were the most easily deluded here, despite the fact that ministers who stayed in the city spoke out against the quacks.

Commentary

The author's own initial acceptance of the portents shows him swayed by common belief, but during the course of the narration we realize that he is one of few people who keeps his head and will not be tricked into believing that he sees something by the hysteria around him. The atmosphere of that hysteria is superbly conveyed. The area of attack is focussed on those who take advantage of a situation for personal profit, a timeless manifestation of the greed inherent in human nature. The strength of the delusions is based upon fear. There are vivid pictures in the narrative, for Defoe is adept at bringing alive the incident or the anecdote, as in the man talking to himself or the woman seeing the angel. The moral indictment of those who print sensational books or set up false advice is a strong one, and once again the Puritan in Defoe is well in evidence. There is some criticism in the miserable type of preaching which does nothing for the people's morale. There is a brief historical retrospect on the recent history of the acts against the Dissenters and, one feels, not a little pride in those dissenting preachers who remain and try to help when their established Anglican brethren ('the incumbents') have fled. The 'oracles of the devil' (p.47) come in for the severest castigation, and the process of advertising fake wares shows that human nature in mid-17th century London had much in common with modern exploitation.

phlegmatic hypochondriac Those who took a gloomy view of everything, convinced that they would suffer the worst.
the conflagration The Fire of London which occurred in 1666.
conjurations Prophecies worked out by star signs.
Lilly's *Almanack*... References to real publications at the time, calculated to excite the responses of the populace. William Lilly's calendar covered the years 1644–81.
Jonah to Nineveh See *Jonah* 3:4–5 'In forty days Nineveh shall be overthrown'.
Josephus Flavius Josephus (?37–?95), Jewish soldier, statesman, became a Roman citizen and wrote a history of the Jews.
palisado Wooden-railed fence.
vapours Depression.
conjunctions The apparent proximity of two heavenly bodies.

dispersers Those who sold them for the printers and publishers.
taken up Arrested.
Persuasions Views, beliefs.
about four years before i.e. the return of Charles II in 1660.
Presbyterians and Independents Protestant sects which were not recognized as part of the Established, Anglican Church.
old channel Pattern, way of behaving.
Nativities i.e. their birth-signs and what they portended.
Friar Bacon's brazen-head See note in Penguin edition, p.47. Bacon (1219–94) was credited with magical powers.
Mother Shipton See note Penguin edition, p.47. Mother Shipton lived in the reign of Henry VIII. She also prophesied the coming of the steam-engine.
habit Garment.
turn me off Sack me.

Revision questions on Sections 1–4

1 In what ways does the author make you feel that you are reading an authentic account of the onset of the Plague? Refer closely to the text in your answer.

2 What do you learn about the character of the narrator from these early sections? Quote in support of your views.

3 What picture do you get of the life of the times from the narrative? Again, use quotations or references or both to illustrate what you say.

4 Write a short essay on (a) quacks and charlatans or (b) the narrator's religious views and beliefs as expressed so far.

5 Write an appreciation of the most interesting or dramatic incident in the narrative so far, giving your reasons for choosing it.

5 up to p.54 'What shall we do?'

Servants were particularly taken advantage of by the quacks. Before the real arrival of the plague the government encouraged prayers as a means of averting the developing catastrophe. Churches and meetings were packed. There was much public confession of sins, but the responsible section of the community prayed sincerely for deliverance. Plays, gambling and other amusements were banned; the effect of this deprivation on the poor was to direct them into the arms of the quacks. Most serious were those who pretended to some knowledge of medicine, and these advertised what they could do. The narrator provides examples of such advertisements. One particular instance given is a direct swindle. There was also the 'wearing charms, philtres, exorcisms, amulets, and I know not what preparations' (p.53) to ward off the plague. He dates the accretion of these lures from about December 1664.

Commentary

This section again shows Defoe through his narrator conveying the temper of the time he is writing about. There is a further attack on the Court, but this is balanced by the behaviour of responsible people in prayer. One gets the feeling that once more Defoe's Puritanism is present when he is writing with some zest about the banning of people's amusements. His account of the power exercised by the opportunist charlatans pretending to have medical knowledge, their advertisements and, above all, the swindling of the poor by the most unscrupulous 'of those quack operators' (p.51) is vivid and direct. He obviously delights in the fact that one man concerned is harassed into compliance by the poor woman standing at his door until he has to give way. Again there is an ironic note in the account of such devices as the word Abracadabra, but a feeling too almost of righteousness (mixed with some compassion) in the fact that all was ineffectual and the poor credulous people were the sufferers. He takes some comfort from the fact that when the plague finally arrived many turned to God in their extremity.

humiliation Repentance.
luxurious See note p.20.
a face of just concern i.e. pretended to be worried.
interludes Dramatic representations.
the manner of the French Court i.e. licentious, lewd – sexual intrigue and court wit are the main ingredients of Restoration comedy in England.
jack-puddings . . . merry andrews Entertainers and clowns, buffoons in shows.
Nineveh See note p.21.
mountebanks Charlatans, fakes.
mercury Used against venereal diseases like syphilis.
subtility Evil cunning.
half-a-crown Equivalent to 12½ pence, but worth very much more then.
almswoman Living in a charitable almshouse.
memorandums Notes on the events – another underlining of the fact that Defoe is aiming at authenticity.
Michaelmas Feast of St Michael, 29 September, a quarter day.
unperforming Not capable of achieving anything.

gulled Swindled.
the first heat i.e. the beginning of the plague in all its force.

6 up to p.67 '1780'

This gives an outline of help for the poor via the Lord Mayor, the magistrates and the College of Physicians. There is another passing reference to the Fire which followed the Plague, and some emphasis on the fact that the Plague resisted all medicines. Physicians were infected and died just as everyone else did. There follows a list of the measures taken according to the narrator. The first is the shutting up of houses (and here there is a historical precedent, for such action was apparently taken during the outbreak of plague at the accession of James I in 1603). The orders take effect from 1st July 1665, examiners being appointed, with their functions described. The narrator then lists the duties of each group – watchmen, searchers of bodies to see whether they died of plague, the chirurgeons (surgeons) to accompany them, the nurse-keepers whose job is to contain the infection. The orders are set out in a straightforward manner, from notification, separation of the diseased, dealing with contaminated belongings, shutting up of houses, keeping anyone within an infected house, the burial of the dead at night, the marking of houses, the issue of certificates by examiners allowing removal, and the regulation about hackney-coaches which have carried people with the plague. There are also orders about the streets, the limitations on assemblies, the forbidding of plays, feasting, 'disorderly tippling in taverns, ale-houses, coffee-houses' (p.65). These in turn are followed by further statistics.

Commentary

This may be called the factual emphasis within the fiction, since here Defoe is drawing on his sources – or adapting them himself – in order to convey the documentary authenticity of what happened. It is completely convincing, for the orders and regulations, however inadequate or abused in the event, are written in the kind of officialese which one would expect and which reads and sounds right. We have the feeling that since the instructions depend so much for their implementation on individual human beings, they are unlikely to be carried out to the letter except in a very few cases. Every now and then the narrator indicates the impractical nature of what is being done.

like the fire Defoe mentions the other great 'visitation', almost as if it goes naturally with the Plague.

were broken i.e. rendered useless.
They endeavoured to do good, and to save the lives of others A good example of the admirable simplicity of Defoe's style.
tokens Signs.
regulation Rational organization and control.
pest-house Hospitals established for plague victims.
Chirurgeons Surgeons.
quartered Housed, found accommodation.
limit Area.
sequestered Separated (and to work only against the plague).
twelvepence One shilling (5p), but worth much more then (see note p.23).
preservatives Drugs (against disease).
aired with fire The smoke and heat would be used (supposedly) to get rid of the infection in the bedclothes, hangings etc.
privity Secret knowledge, legal assent.
six feet deep See note in Penguin edition, p.62. The minimum depth for graves.
criers and carriers Men who go about the streets advertising the wares they have for sale.
a red cross The standard, recognized sign of infection within.
the rakers Those who swept up the rubbish.
Laystalls Refuse heaps.
tippling-houses Public houses.
buckler-play Fencing.
dispersing Spreading.

7 up to p.76 '... expected in such cases'

The main topic here is the effects of the shutting up of houses. This was sometimes done needlessly, and on the face of it appears very cruel. People of course tried to get out of the situation, particularly if they were – as yet – uninfected. The first story involves watchmen who eventually enter an infected house, find a woman dead, and realize that everybody else has succeeded in getting out and have left her to die. Various other devices for escaping are described. There is the tale of the man and his family escaping although their door was marked with a cross because a servant had the plague. Violence against watchmen was commonplace. These escapes inevitably led to the spread of infection. The story of the mother and daughter shows how suddenly the plague struck, and the terrible reactions that it produced.

Commentary

Defoe is here on his favourite ground, the stories and anecdotes, the observations and the graphic narration of the supposed eye-witness of the horrors. The switch from the factual to the incidents which illustrate the extremities endured makes for dramatic narrative tension. The expectation of the reader is aroused. What will be the end of each story? What will human nature descend to, rise to, be victim of? Defoe is, too, a master at moving the reader by the sheer contemplation of suffering, mainly because we are always aware of his own involvement and compassion. <u>The writing is simple, graphic, direct, compelling.</u>

causelessly Without good reason.
distempered Made sick.
But it was a public good that justified the private mischief Note the antithetical balance and economy of this expression.
stratagem Cunning device.
of which by itself i.e. examples follow.
which he was to stay for the making up Which he had to wait for.
true in the general Note how Defoe qualifies his statement – he is not recording accurately, but telling stories which are true in the essence if not true in fact. The whole narrative is therefore a symbol of what happened.
usage Treatment.
warding and watching Guarding and defending.
exigencies Urgent needs or acts.
catched Caught (archaic).
miscarried i.e. were killed by the plague.
is not to be expressed i.e. there aren't words to describe.
give her things to sweat Make her sweat to bring out the fever.
three of those watchmen were publicly whipped Note the severity of the punishment, which has as its aim the salutary lesson for others – setting up more fear if they should go against the regulations.

8 up to p.90 '11th of July to the 18th'

Here Defoe starts as if he is going to tell the story of the three men, and then appears to think better of it, having first indicated that the reader may find something salutary in the story. He returns to the actual practices which obtained during the pestilence, giving some account of the great pit dug at Aldgate. There is a supposedly direct account of the burials contingent upon the raging fever of September. People are forbidden to go to this and other large pits, but some in the grip of the disease run to them and throw themselves in anyway. The narrator gets admittance through the sexton, who tells him that the experience will be as good as a sermon to him. His first story is of the distracted man there whose family are dead in the cart. He is taken to a tavern, while the narrator describes the terrible sights in the burial ground. There are various stories about the buriers robbing the dead and the cruelty of the nurses. The next account is of the tavern where the man was taken. The latter suffers abuse, as does the narrator, from the unprincipled group who drink there. The narrator is abused for his godly views, but he learns that within a fortnight they all die of the Plague. He is horrified by their blasphemy, but after his anger has subsided he determines to pray for them. He returns to the subject of the watchmen and how they are abused, and again comments on the shutting up of houses. This section concludes with the man who broke out of his house and dies in the garret of an inn, thus infecting the occupants.

Commentary

The vividness of the narration about the pits which were dug and the throwing in of the bodies sustains the horror, but as always with Defoe it is the individual story, visual, moving, powerful, which is the cornerstone of his art. The tavern scene is reminiscent of the rioters' tavern scene in Chaucer's *The Pardoner's Tale*, and there is the same stern moral lesson to be drawn from it. The pathos of the man symbolizes the suffering of the many families, while the narrator shows his true christianity by (a) having the courage to stand up to the drinkers and (b) having the Christian charity to pray for them. He is never less than human, having the curiosity, and courage, to risk his own life by seeing the bodies thrown into the pit. He admits that what he sees is 'such as no tongue can express' (p.79). He captures the general hysteria, the terror, the anguish. There is moving contrast between the manly grief of the man whose family are dead and the vicious, abusive insensitivity of the revellers in the tavern. In fact the narrator's going to the tavern indicates Christian concern for the poor unfortunate. He shows good reason and control in dealing with the revellers. He thinks his way through what they have said and done until his faith tells him that he must 'pray for those who despitefully used me' (p.87). He repeats his practical view that the shutting up of houses only led to a greater spreading of the plague because it made people escape and infect others. The account of the man of superior class who dies in the garret is a small masterpiece, the incident again being used to symbolize the way the plague was spread. There is the now common factual statistics and exact dates to authenticate the occurrences.

laid up Saved.
my curiosity Note the disarming way this is acknowledged. Despite his strong Christian principles, the narrator makes the occasion of the Plague an excuse for sensation-seeking.

links Bearers of torches of pitch and tow used to light the cart along the streets.
bellman A man who attracted attention by ringing a bell – normally a town crier, but here obviously signalling the death-cart and warning people to stay in.
promiscuously i.e. without care or concern.
loose Loosely clothed, or having merely a sheet.
to pray for those who despitefully used me An echo of the collect embodying the principles of the Sermon on the Mount according to Luke (6:29).
entertained Provided.
trained bands Companies of citizen-soldiers organized in London in the 16th, 17th and 18th centuries.
relations Accounts.
commit the charge Give the responsibility.

Revision questions on Sections 5–8

1 Indicate the range of the tricks practised by the quacks in order to get the custom of ordinary people.

2 Indicate the main measures imposed by the Lord Mayor through the magistrates, and say what effect these had.

3 Give an account of two episodes arising from the shutting up of houses.

4 What seems to you the most terrible incident in this section and why?

5 What do you learn of burying and burial-grounds from this section?

6 In what ways would you regard the narrator's actions as courageous in this section? You should refer to the text in your answer.

9 up to p.100 'and saw the tokens'

A further account of those who fled, including details on how some of the well-to-do people coped with the situation. The narrator notes that often the infection was transmitted by servants, who had to go out into the infected areas to get provisions and the like for their employers. The practical nature of the writer is seen in his bemoaning the fact that there was only one pest-house to which people could be sent. The spread, too, was largely due to the ignorance and selfishness of people, and the narrator himself admits that he himself was guilty of sending servants out and thus contributing to their risk and his own. From time to time inevitably he regrets that he has not left London, and he determines not to venture out in the streets again. For three or four days he writes his notes and 'private meditations' (p.94). He is friendly with a physician, Dr Heath, and as a result of his advice he begins to bake his own bread and to lay in provisions, since he feels that people irresponsibly going about is the ruination of the city. He notes again almost in passing that the infection was spread through food and in markets: he notes people dead in the street, and this reinforces his determination to lock himself up with his 'family' and food and see the plague out that way. But of course he is still responsible for going to his brother's house, and records the terrible sights and sounds he hears from within houses as the plague approaches a peak. There follows some detail on the nature of the swellings in the disease, the distraction and madness that frequently attends it, and the fact that some died easily hardly knowing that they had the disease. There was a feeling that if the swelling broke, the infection would disperse and the patient would recover.

Commentary

The psychological effect of being shut up in a house with someone who is infected is given considered stress, but the factual account of how the infection spread has, it must be acknowledged, all the advantages of hindsight. In a way this contributes to the truth of what is being said, for it is surely human nature to be wise after the event. Defoe takes some delight in this kind of rational appraisal, so that the reader feels that (Defoe) knows and is really something of an authority. He concludes that the infection is from body to body. The lack of foresight over going out is also stressed, but the implied comment is that people are slow to change their habits, even when crisis is upon them. One of the main aspects of this chapter is the concentration on the *pain* which the plague causes (both physical and emotional) and the *fear* engendered in the author himself. Here Defoe employs the cunning device of mentioning his prayers, his private meditations and his writing down a record of what he saw, another strand in the rope of supposed authenticity. Throughout we get the impression that the narrator is a devout man. His advice from Dr Heath and his practical application of it in providing for himself and his servants shows a marked sense of responsibility and practical ability. The precautions in the butchers' stalls are emphatic of authentic detail, while the country people coming to the fringe of the city and selling their produce there shows that the authorities were at least alive to the dangers. With the increase in the violence of the plague there is a corresponding increase in the reactions of the populace – madness, suicide. Defoe takes some delight, we feel, in detailed description of the swellings. The fact that he is a reporter (supposedly) and not really a sensationalist is shown by the way he relates the virtually painless and unexpected deaths of the plague by way of contrast.

out of question to me Beyond any doubt.
enthusiasm Excessive bias.
dismal objects Upsetting sights.
made themselves away Committed suicide.
What I wrote of my private meditations... Defoe has the habit of tantalizing the reader. Yet the idea of having something in reserve helps to authenticate the account.
rozen Resin.
dreadfully visited Experienced the plague terribly.
vitals Heart, lungs etc.
general articles Main lists or reports.
running out of their own government Losing control of themselves.
particular Sign, indication.

10 up to p.117 'the account is exactly true'

The cruelty of human nature, even to murder and of course to looting and robbery, is recorded, some of the thieves taking clothes from the bodies as well as rings and jewellery. The narrator considers that the women were the chief offenders. But he does not altogether accept the truth of some of the stories, which were from distant parts of the town and could thus not be verified. A succession of stories testifies to individual suffering. On one occasion he sees women coming from near his brother's house wearing hats. Many of them have seen fit to help themselves. His remonstration with the women is in vain. The particular story of the gravedigger and the piper is next told, the narrator being sure of its general truth though doubtful of the embellishments in the telling. He next discusses the decision to bury people well away from the city, the lack of any proper preparations for the plague, and the fact that there were a number of charitable payments to relieve the suffering of the poor. Even those who fled, including the King, made these payments. He then sets out in documentary form the main trades and occupations of those who suffered. In simple terms, the narrator's own, 'all trades being stopped, employment ceased: the labour, and by that the bread, of the poor were cut off' (p.112). These poor were greatly helped by payments from the Lord Mayor and his Aldermen and the Justices of the Peace. The mob in any case had nothing much to steal, since there were few provisions stored up. Servants were found jobs as watchmen and nurses, yet there were so many poor that in a sense it was a deliverance that the plague killed them. Again details of totals are provided. But it is the narrator's private opinion that the plague killed 100,000 in the year as distinct from the 68,500 who were officially listed, and many died outside in the country.

Commentary

The crimes committed, some of which the author does not believe, are described with the author's customary vividness. We are aware of his compassion and charity here. He is really intent on exposing the slanderous nature of rumour as distinct from fact, what is verifiable. He obviously believes in the goodness of the Lord Mayor and many of his colleagues. The hat incident is imbued with natural humour, not without irony in view of the fact that (a) the author is very serious and (b) the women may not live long enough to enjoy what they have stolen. Even here he is charitable – 'I considered that this was not a time to be cruel and rigorous' (p.105). Very good indeed is the story of John Hayward (again it reflects the author's belief in Providence). 'The piper' is perhaps the finest anecdote in the novel, and again, reasonably rare in Defoe, the humour in this deathly incident is noteworthy. It is told in a racy and uncontrived manner, and it is not overstated by adding in embellishments. There is again some praise for those who assisted the poor, but a bitter aside that the same charitable monies were not forthcoming the following year to replace buildings destroyed in the fire. His compassion shines through in his account of the state of the poor, but one also gets the impression that (a) he accepts the divine providence to such an extent that he regards the killing off of so many of the poor as a form of deliverance and (b) that he is inclined to over-praise what was done in terms of relief. The section closes with a moving account of his occasional excursions to the fields of Bethnal Green and Hackney – again this insatiable curiosity provides him with the material of his narrative.

rational To be likely.
come at Obtain.
'death in his face' Note the vivid economy and immediacy of the phrase.
'Forsooth' Truly, in truth.
upon another foot i.e. adopting another approach.
in form i.e. buried, taken to the burial, in a particular way.
tied Confined.
Chamber of London The government of London.

Compter Debtors' prison.
Monument Column erected 11 years after the Great Fire (1666).
the liberty of Westminster See note Penguin edition, p.110.
report Rumour.
so lively a case Such an established fact.
merchandising Trade and commerce.
caulkers Those who stop up the seams in a ship.
substance i.e. what they possessed.
dismal article Tragic circumstance.
more particular to this part Say much more about this.
tumults Riots.
took off Killed.
within a trifle Very nearly.
at all hazards Despite all risks.
out of the compass of the communication Beyond the reach of the authorities, so that they could not be included in the bills of mortality.

11 up to p.137 'But I shall come to this part again'

An account of the streets, many major ones with grass growing in the middle of them. It was a particularly bad time at the beginning of September for the devastating effects of the disease, but it never got completely out of hand, so 'that it was never to be said of London that the living were not able to bury the dead' (p.119). Much roaring, crying, and the denunciations of one Solomon Eagle were heard. The narrator indicates that there was some worship at the worst of times, and praises God that he himself was spared. He reports the incident of the precautions taken to ensure that a purse of money was not infected, and then gives an account of walking out into the fields towards Bow. There follows the story of the man who brings provisions in his boat for his wife and family, but dare not go near them. He expresses his own simple Christian faith, and is much moved when the narrator gives him money to help relieve his family. He learns that the plague has reached some of the ships at Greenwich, but his view of these ships makes him feel that those on board are protected from the worst effects of the disease, though some died and were thrown overboard into the river. He points out that many people living in Redriff, Wapping, Ratcliff and Limehouse were lulled into a sense of false security, and that when it overtook them the plague was devastating. He notes that the idea of saving oneself became the first priority, so that some parents even killed their children. Particularly terrible, he notes, was the plight of women about to give birth to a child, since most of the midwives were either dead or fled. Again more statistics are provided. Some of the recently born children starved because they could not be fed, others went on sucking breasts that were already dead. Children infected mothers and nurses and vice versa. Some of the effects on those suffering extreme grief are also catalogued. The final part of this section, before the story of the three men is told, gives an account of the necessary killing of all cats and dogs.

Commentary

There is the usual emphasis here on the fact that the bills of mortality did not tell the whole story. The narrative deals with the desolation in September with a frightening realism, but still with a sense of pride that those in authority never ceased to make sure that everything that could be done was done. There is the grotesque account of Solomon Eagle 'with a pan of burning charcoal on his head' (p.119), though one feels at times that Defoe is unconsciously rather than deliberately humorous. The author's (narrator's) own mood changes as one might expect in the crisis – sometimes he stays in and sometimes he goes out. One feels too his sense of loyalty to those Dissenters who stayed and prayed. His own sensitivity is seen in the fact that he still hears and sees in his mind what happened then. The incident of the fumigating of the purse, together with the eerie effect of the silence in the streets, shows Defoe's command of atmosphere. Curiosity carries him away towards Greenwich and the ships, for he is always intent upon discovery. The story of the poor man and his devotion to his family is pathetic; though it is moving, the dialogue hardly sounds true to life, and we sense that this is symbolic representation in praise of goodness and simplicity. It also has the effect of bringing out the genuine charitable concern of the narrator, and a direct move towards finding out about the ships. More statistics are deployed, there is some comment on human failings at this time of distress, 'self-preservation, indeed, appeared here to be the first law' (p.130), though the narrator is generally inclined to treat human weakness with tolerance and charity. The emphasis on child suffering and infection is one of the most <u>harrowing</u> in the novel. The reference to the slaughter of animals is another of those practical details which contribute to the <u>veracity</u> of the journal.

people generally went in the middle A graphic illustration of the fear of the plague.
quicken Stimulate.
Solomon Eagle (1618–83). Musician, a fanatical quaker at the time.

enthusiast One who is obsessed.
could not hold it Could not keep it up.
post-house From where horses would set off with the letters.
hazard Risk.
he goes Note the use of the present tense to make the incident more vivid to the reader.
groats A silver coin worth four pence, but only in current usage until 1662, 3 years before the Plague.
Redriff Rotherhithe.
the Pool The part of the Thames immediately below London Bridge.
just to him i.e. being fair to him.
attended ship affairs Worked on the river and on board the ships.
insensibly Without their knowledge.
strange temper Odd behaviour.
Dullege, and Lusum Dulwich and Lewisham.
hoys, smacks Large and small sailing vessels.
rid at their roads While they were riding at anchor.
every one's private safety lay so near them . . . Notice that Defoe deplores the concern with self.
all bowels of love Compassion.
I shall not take upon me to vouch the truth . . . Note this disclaimer, appropriate in a work of fiction.
to lay them Prepare them to give birth.
travail Labour, childbirth.
chrisoms Children who had just been baptized.
Woe be to those who are with child . . . Defoe is deliberately employing a tone which has scriptural echoes because of the widespread infant mortality rate.
starved at nurse Died while being fed, the milk being either non-existent or the person diseased.
stupid Rendered dumbfounded, out of their wits.
like an armed man This simile is unusual for Defoe, who does not employ a great deal of imagery, but this is menacingly effective.
Wherefore For which reason.
Providence concurring With the agreement of God, a further instance of Defoe's reverence for the divine will.

12 up to p.164 'back again to London'

This is the narrative of the three men, earlier mentioned on pp.76–7 and then dropped, who initially do not know what to do. After discussion they decide to venture into the country to escape the Plague. They even debate the legal position with regard to themselves as vagrants. Two of them are turned out of their lodgings anyway, so that they have no alternative but to go. They set off after the middle of July, making practical arrangements. Their journey is traced in some detail, though Defoe himself turns aside from them momentarily to give a brief account of the Plague raging in August. They camp by a great barn near Hackney, and are joined by a large travelling group who are good, sober (and religious) people and who are seeking security just as they are. They discuss the situation among themselves. The three men decide to follow this group into Essex. They are denied entrance to Walthamstow. John the soldier talks with the constable, and they get food sent out to them, though they must stay outside, for the inhabitants are fearful that they bring the infection, which other groups have done. After a day or so they set off for Epping. John gets food from the market, but again they remain outside. When people come to look at them they are afraid, for already there are rumours that the plague is at Waltham. There is a debate with the Epping people, who have news of what happened at Walthamstow. John's rational power of argument influences the Epping men, and they are given food and straw. With the aid of the carpenter they build a dwelling and stay there until September, when they hear that the plague 'was very hot' (p.159) at Waltham Abbey. They grind their corn near Woodford, but they learn that the towns around are infected, and other people begin to go into the country to escape this. Unfortunately some of them did not get out quickly enough. John and the group have to move, but they are given a certificate. They consider Waltham and then Hainault, but eventually decide to encamp on their old site again before returning to London in December.

Commentary

To use the narrator's own words of the story of the three men, 'Their story has a moral in every part of it' (p.137). Set in the structure of *A Journal*, it is a story within the story, and, though lively and immediate, is rather in the style of a moral fable like *The Pilgrim's Progress* than an account of real people in a real situation; the dialogue, for instance, does not ring true. It subserves the Defoe theme of illustrating how certain people may have behaved in adversity, but is idealized because for the most part it is so reasonable and so practical. The dialogue form however, set out initially as in a play, gives an immediacy of experience, so that we feel that we are with the characters as they take their decisions. John the soldier is a natural leader and organizer, and has some of the most tellingly moral lines in the whole exchange – 'the whole kingdom is my native country as well as this town' – and, even more forcefully, 'I was born in England, and have a right to live in it if I can' (p.139). This assertion of freedom is not born of fear. We note the communal resolve and decision, the practicality of the sailmaker becoming tentmaker. The travellers need all their wits about them and have to lie and deceive in order to get what they need and go where they want. Moral: you have to be cunning to survive. We feel the pressures of the time in their having to obtain certificates. There is a kind of generalized Christian idealism present in the fact that they meet a good group of people, and once more there is an emphasis on 'the blessing and direction of Providence' (p.147). The atmosphere of insecurity is well conveyed, evidence the rumours in Epping that the Plague was in Waltham and 'that there had been a great rabble of people at Walthamstow' (p.156) who were, of course, in fact this small group of refugees from London. Again we feel that the details being given have the stamp of authenticity. The dialogue with the constable is almost too reasonable to be true, but the movements, the fears, the reasoning, the do-it-yourself devices to which they are put, make it a good, exciting, and sometimes moving story. There is something of an anti-climax to it, for Defoe – or rather the narrator – is really working towards explaining the return to the city of people in great numbers once the fever had abated. He has also sufficiently conveyed the fear in the country at large, both about the plague and about catching it from people fleeing from London.

distracted Very upset.
the Low Countries The Netherlands.
stated Situated.
warned out . . . quite out Warned to go . . . had to leave.
husbands People who are thrifty and economical.
a fig Anything of no value.
good hap Good fortune.
rope-walk Long piece of ground used for twisting rope.
fetched a long compass Took a long way round.
at this loose rate Casually, without taking precautions.
upon the scout On the lookout.
parley Discussion.
intelligence News.
commit spoil Do damage.
this was doing Going on.
upon sufferance Subject to permission.
we shall make ourselves the better allowance We shall take more.
to quarter upon us Live with us, taking our food.
raise the county Call up the other constables, soldiers etc.
asunder Separated.
discover Give them away.
fix their stand Stay put.
Rumford Romford.

a great charge Heavy cost.
kept retired Stayed apart.
coverlids Covers to put over themselves.
was very hot Intense.
higlers Pedlars.
time enough Quickly enough.
retired from all conversation for above forty days Like Christ in the wilderness – a deliberate echo here.
signal Sign, evidence.
Henalt Hainault.
great straits Severe distress.

Revision questions on Sections 9–12

1 Give what details you can about the nature of the plague and how, in the opinion of the narrator, it was spread.

2 Indicate the influence on the narrator of Dr Heath, and say what he did as a result of this influence.

3 Write an account of either (a) the hats incident or (b) the story of the piper.

4 Write an account of the sufferings of the poor, indicating what steps were taken to relieve their distress during this period.

5 In what ways do you think the author shows his own compassion and concern in these sections?

6 Give some account of the story of the man who brings provisions for his family by boat.

7 Explain why the three men of Wapping behave as they do, and say what the story tells you about human nature in this kind of crisis.

13 up to p.187 'it would be their last'

Continuation of how the poor sought relief in the countryside, how the ships did not get the plague, how the watermen were able to conduct themselves away. There is a story of a man who gets a house in another area but is not allowed to stay. There follow some statistics of death from plague in towns around London. There are further remarks on how the poor seemed to wilfully infect the poor, and how any propensity to loot, rob or riot was killed off almost before it began. And this in turn is succeeded by another indictment of the problems caused by and the incidents arising from the shutting up of houses.

The narrator gives an example of a woman confined with spots only, and all others were shut up with her. These others became sick of various ailments anyway as a result of being confined. The narrator is appointed an examiner, tells the story of the gentlewoman kissed in the street by the delirious man with the Plague. He then argues for the shutting up of houses in order to prevent the spread by street infection. The most remarkable story is that of the man who swims across the Thames and back and rids himself of the infection as a result. At first the order for shutting up houses was not strictly enforced. People drowned themselves, but these deaths were not included in the weekly bills of mortality. The magistrates could not effectively prevent people from walking in the streets. He summarizes the difficulties of examiners in getting at the truth, since cases were concealed and lying became commonplace. The narrator got himself discharged from his onerous responsibilities after three weeks. But at the height of the plague no houses were shut up at all. The sights of madness and delirium had a morally debilitating effect. Fires were used by some to try to kill off the disease, but the Lord Mayor had them stopped. August and September saw the height of the plague, with people once contaminated dying in a very short time. Bodies were left to rot, but those still alive went to the churches without taking any heed of who was next to them. They felt that they were doomed.

Commentary

The pathos of numbers dying in the countryside unaccounted for and unidentified is the theme of the first section here. The atmosphere of panic is sustained, the poor man having his belongings removed an instance of it. More statistics are given for the outer areas. The narrator dwells on that facet of human nature which caused people to behave wickedly and infect others, with more praise of the Lord Mayor and his magistrates and more criticism of the shutting up of houses. Conflicts between watchmen and those shut up underline the frustrations and abuses. Again the examples given, like that of the maid shut up in the house in Whitechapel, are vivid in their particularity. But the narrator sees clearly in his rational two-way debate that the consequences attendant upon letting people roam about with the infection would have increased the spread of the plague. The swimming the Thames incident shows the narrator (Defoe) at his best; note the economy and effectiveness of the story. Street scenes are graphic and immediate. Always we are aware of the religious man behind the writing, for instance shown in his thankfulness that no outbreaks of fire made things worse. He is explicit and straightforward about the difficulties facing examiners and about his own distaste for the task given both the danger and unpopularity of the job. (He only continues in his task for three weeks.) The general atmosphere of increasing hopelessness is well conveyed. The emphasis on people dying suddenly shows the unremitting nature of the plague.

in the offing Positioned at a distance from the shore.
stocks Wooden construction in which a person could be imprisoned by the ankles.
popular Widespread.
maugre Despite.
Cum aliis With others; i.e. many more died.
observed by him i.e. his favourites, those he had taken to.
in the colours they were described in As it was so presented (the implication here is of distortion).
he was continued Kept in office.
insensibly See note p.34.
scorbutic Scurvy.
order Prescription, title.
would not answer the end Would not achieve the desired results.
abatement Relief, satisfaction.
hurry Panic.
aught Anything.
probity Integrity, honesty.
as with a bullet that killed with the stroke Rare image, trying to convey the suddenness.
concerted Conspired, agreed.
egress and regress Going out and coming in.
the fire the succeeding year Yet another mention of the second catastrophe, and a reinforcement of the narrator's view of Divine Providence.
caustics Having burning or corrosive powers.
dog-days Period of July and August during the rising of Sirius the dog-star, thought to be the hottest and most unhealthy period of the year.
touched Had the signs of the plague.
all go All die.

14 up to p.206 'that was infected before'

This opens with the theme that people put aside sectarian differences during the period of crisis, and asserts that if there were another plague year it would again bring people together. The narrator asks what more he can say when he has given the instances of the man setting fire to himself in bed and the other running naked in the streets, of the sufferings of the people? He speaks of remaining much at home, then gives a terrible picture of the death-carts waiting. He notes the vanishing of the quacks before proceeding to the statistics of September, which was the worst month of all. Again he suggests that the number of deaths is far below the true total, and then instances the actions taken by the magistrates in this period. All bodies were buried, the level of food supplies was maintained. He remarks the efficiency of the pest-houses (while wishing that there had been more). There follows a step back to the beginning of the plague, with the plans made then, and the constraints placed on people like constables and churchwardens to remain in the city. All that was unpleasant – the conveying of the dead for example – was done at night. There is a brief survey of the movement of the Plague, together with the effects in terms of rumours on the rest of the country. Again, statistics are supplied to show the decrease in the number of burials. There are further accounts, which he admits are repetitious, of the sufferings of the city.

Commentary

The genuine Christianity of the narrator comes across in his attack on religious differences and the need for there to be positive Christian action at a time of crisis. He will not set himself up to judge, he says philosophically, but laments the fact that 'we cannot be content to go hand in hand to the place where we shall join heart and hand' (p.189). There is more graphic account of distress and the atmosphere of death, the carts looming over everything. The narrator's faith is seen in the fact that divine Providence sorts out the fakes and charlatans of all kinds. There is a frightening visual atmosphere with the dead-carts unloaded, but the narrator's own practicality is seen in the fact that he believes that there should be more pest-houses. The achievements of the Lord Mayor and magistrates show the narrator once more well-disposed towards them in gratitude for what organization there was. This appears to be because he understands the psychological need to keep up morale, and believes that the authorities did this by the quality of their organization. He still continues cynical about the accuracy of the bills of mortality. The invidious nature of the Plague is fully spelled out. The carrying of it through the air is mentioned, but the narrator's return to the power of Providence is this time to indicate the number of people who did not succumb to the plague, but were delivered from it.

Act of Uniformity The act of 1662 prescribing the use of one Book of Common Prayer. It was directed against the Puritans.
breaches are fomented i.e. differences are stirred up.
Another plague year would reconcile all these differences One of the most telling statements in the whole book.
getting great estates Making immense profits from which they would buy extensive property.
calculate their own nativities Work out their fortunes from their own birth-signs.
with lenity Generously, mercifully.
the Lord Mayor ... Common Council The corporation which consisted of the Lord Mayor, his aldermen, his council men elected from the wards.
assize Statutory price (of bread).
reputation Rumour.
abstract Summary.
a faithful monitor A direct indication.
disturbed Contaminated.
Turkish predestinarianism The acceptance of fate common in the East.

15 up to p.220 'the direction of Divine Providence by that means'

The narrator now undertakes a survey of what happened, with inevitably some repetition. He summarizes the unconscious spreading of the infection, giving the example of the optimist in September who thinks he has survived it all but in fact already has the marks upon him. He does not know how long the plague can remain dormant within one, but gives the direct opinion that the best way to avoid the plague is to run away from it. He has ideas of separating people into smaller units living less close together in an attempt to stop the devastating spread. There is one story of an employer who sacrifices himself for others when he learns he has the plague. He gives instances of the delusory nature of the plague where people not knowing that they have it, have inadvertently passed it on. In a fine phrase Defoe describes one of these as 'a walking destroyer' (p.213). Diagnosis was difficult. Various views held by physicians as to the means of detection are given. He also goes into time, from the first plague victim in December 1664 and the delusory recession of the disease in February to April the following year. But many who died during this period, notified as having done so from other causes, could have had the plague. Gradually it was born in upon people that the disease could be passed on inadvertently. This led to caution in human contact, but with the first onset there was much public prayer.

Commentary

The historical basis is again stressed. There is some shrewd analysis and examples of people unknowingly infecting one another, which gives a strange irony to the whole devastation. The tone of rational discussion, with respect for the conclusions of the physicians, is maintained throughout. There is as always some fine direct writing ('the best physic against the plague is to run away from it', p.209). There is the usual commonsense in arriving at the conclusion that overcrowding facilitated the spread of the plague. The analogy is cunningly linked with the onset and spread of the fire in the following year. There are the usual insights into motives and attitudes which show the basis for human behaviour. The good side of human nature is often stressed, as with the man who had himself removed from his family and spoke to them only at a distance so that they should not be contaminated. The capacity for people's deluding themselves is also revealed. H.F. also gives some account of the terrible distortions of the imagination. The narrative rests much on the advantages of hindsight, which gives the narrator the opportunity to draw conclusions not evident at the time but which appear obvious later. The precautions to ward off the plague – like talking to strangers at a distance and having 'preservatives in their mouths' (p.219) – show that some people kept their heads and in doing so saved themselves and others.

foundation point Beginning.
backward Not open or forthcoming.
confounded Confused, made worse.
propagation Spreading.
the arrow flies thus unseen The arrow is normally associated with Cupid's bow and love; here it is used ironically and with fatal effect in terms of the plague.
roupy Suffering from a disease which affects poultry and which generally ends in death.
several other articles which bore a proportion A number of other things which were related to this.
imposthumes, gripes Abscesses and stomach pains.
spotted fever See note p.17.
shy and jealous Cautious and protective.
took with i.e. the infection was transmitted.
preservatives See note p.25.
(with due reserve to the direction of Divine Providence) i.e. implying that they were saved because of the precautions that they took but also because God willed it.

16 up to p.233 'after the fire of London'

A comment on the behaviour of the poor who were often foolhardy and irresponsible, and on the charitable relief they received. Great praise for charity given by the rich, with further praise to God for his moving their hearts with compassion. Some detail is then given on the reduction, almost to the point of non-existence, of trade, though there were reports that English ships had carried the plague into a number of other countries. He notes that the spread and distortion of rumour abroad was greater than the plague itself. Countries like Flanders and Holland, with whom England was at war, were able to take full advantage of this. But various English towns not affected by the Plague were able to export for a time until the infection spread. Only in August and September, at the height, did no ships deliver cargoes to England. The corn and coal trades were maintained throughout, though the incursions of the Dutch did prevent some of the supplies getting through from Newcastle. Public fires were built to try to halt the spread of the infection. The narrator next notes the general adequacy of food and provisions during the period of the Plague, though exports were hit as a result of the dying down of all employment in the City. The poor were affected throughout England because of the collapse of the manufacturing industries in London.

Commentary

Although there is some compassion in his account of the sufferings of the poor, there is also considerable adverse comment as well, the implication being that they were too ignorant to learn anything. There is the usual praise of those who gave charitable aid, with the rather naive assertion that he knew of none of them who caught the disease. This is another plus mark for human nature – and Divine Providence – as far as the narrator is concerned. The practical commercial man (which Daniel Defoe of course was) comes to the fore; the narrator is very aware of the effects of the plague on trade. In addition, such detail conveys a flavour of authenticity in the narrative. The registering of rumour and its effects abroad is natural, but the evaluation of the spread of the Plague all over the kingdom leads one to think that the narrator is again apportioning blame to all those who moved about freely during the time of distress. We note that the burning of the fires on the advice of physicians was particularly interesting as a means of containing the contagion. The narrator himself obviously believes in the efficacy of such action. Again the caution with regard to the delivery of coal is praised. Another

44 A Journal of the Plague Year

interesting underlining of the Providence theme is seen in the narrator's concern with the fire the following year – the fact that manufacturing industry was now needed to supply the needs of the citizens in terms of clothes, furniture etc. in the half-destroyed city.

miscarried Died.
the islands of the Arches Greek islands in the Mediterranean.
Smyrna and Scanderoon Turkish ports.
kerseys Cloths which are coarse, usually ribbed.
lost nothing in the carriage Was not diminished by being carried everywhere.
conversing Mixing.
land-carriage Conveyed overland.
capers See note, Penguin edition p.230. Remember England was at war with the Dutch, hence the reference to 'the States' in the same paragraph.
chalder Coal measure. A chauldron = 36 bushels.
since that experiment i.e. lighting the fires to combat the Plague.
a quick vent i.e. outlet for supplies.

17 up to the end

The narrator is told by Dr Heath that the plague will now die down. This begins towards the end of September. The narrator summarizes the figures in October. In fact 'the malignity of the disease abated' (p.234). People go about more, many catch it, caustics are applied, and physicians advise cautious movement among the people. There is a further complication, for many return to the city who have fled into the country, with the result that the bills of mortality go up again in November – witness the story of the barber John Cock and his household. The reaction towards licentious behaviour after deliverance from the Plague amounted to something approaching hysteria. The king now issued commands about the relief of the poor. New burial-grounds were made, including one specially set aside for Quakers. Physicians and ministers who had abandoned their posts now found themselves much abused on their return. The narrator reveals that he is of the orthodox church, but condemns the ousting of Dissenters from the pulpits they had entered at the time of crisis. Old animosities are resumed. Many boast unwisely that they stayed. The narrator recalls that he did little or nothing himself to preserve himself from the Plague. He did however take his friend Heath's advice by using Venice treacle (see note below). He observes the disappearance of the quacks, though prophecies that the Plague would return were common. By February health has been generally restored in London, though some people still burnt perfumes etc. against the return of the

Plague. The fleet was not infected, and though many had been impressed into it this was obviously the saving of their lives. The final sections of the narrative are an invocation in praise of God who alone could have saved the City. There was no miracle cure. The narrator says that even the doctors 'were obliged to acknowledge that it was all supernatural, that it was extraordinary, and that no account could be given of it' (p.254). The common people often thanked God in the streets for saving them. These streets were sometimes full with bandaged people who were recovering. The final stanza is a mark of the narrator's thankfulness at being spared.

Commentary

Heath, based probably on the doctor Hodges who wrote an account of the Plague in Latin prior to the publication of *A Journal of the Plague Year*, shows his wisdom and good judgment. Even more telling is the account of people's reactions; previously cautious, the moment the disaster appears to recede they are deluded into taking unnecessary risks. There is a realistic description of the treatment of swellings. It is quite typical of a generative hysteria that people should take little or no notice of the doctors. The wish to return to their homes is so strong that many indulge it and die as a result. The author, however, takes a tolerant view of the stories that the people indulged in excesses. He is always tolerant on broad issues, possibly because of his faith. Another interesting and accurate comment is seen in the narrator's reporting that once the plague was over charitable provisions stopped. This is typical of human nature after crisis. There is a terrible realism, too, in the exhumation of bodies and their movement to new burial grounds; it is almost as if the evidence of the plague lives on. There is an aftermath of gruesomeness and opportunism which is disturbing. Another aspect of the revenge motive in human nature is seen in the anger directed against doctors, ministers too, who deserted their charges. The fact that once a crisis is over the dissensions which preceded it come back with just the same potency is also true to life. Again we are aware of the narrator's tolerance and generosity of spirit:

A plague is a formidable enemy, and is armed with terrors that every man is not sufficiently fortified to resist or prepared to stand the shock against. It is very certain that a great many of the clergy who were in circumstances to do it withdrew and fled for the safety of their lives; but 'tis true also that a great many of them stayed, and many of them fell in the calamity and in the discharge of their duty. (p.244)

Again the narrator notes the extremes of reaction, like damning those who left and boasting about staying themselves. He puts the moral and religious view that he would rather have seen from people much more charity and kindness than idle boasting. The level-headedness of the narrator is shown in his own sparse use of 'preventative' measures against the disease, and, of course, his disgust at all the charlatans and quacks who tried to take advantage of the crisis. One of the fascinating aspects of this narrative towards the end is the incidents and rumours and prophecies which, so to speak, keep the pot of the Plague boiling.

The narrator's view is an unequivocal one: deliverance comes from God, and that is why he and others were saved. In one of his rare images he observes that 'the poison was taken out of the sting' (p.254). He has the sensitivity to realize that there is something offensive in his going on to preach a sermon, and so he refrains. His examples of people in the street have something of idealization about them, but throughout we have been impressed by his sincerity, his powers of observation and his honesty. If there are repetitious sequences in the account, we should perhaps bear in mind that the plague itself was repetitious. The first to die were the tokens of the many in the unremitting destruction of human life.

humour Mood, practice, whim.
like seamen after a storm is over Rare image, but it echoes the situation of Robinson Crusoe.
Mahometans ... predestination A favourite Defoe reference – see note p.34.
abandoned effects Belongings which were left.
the main occasion i.e. the real crisis.
stopped their hands i.e. did not continue contributing.
shy of us Wary, cautious.
physic garden Where herbs used in cures and treatments were grown.
Sir Robert Clayton Whig politician who became Lord Mayor of London in 1679.
thronged Fine choice of word = crowded or over-crowded.
a doctor to be let A pun, meaning (a) bled or (b) there is a vacancy here (because of his absence during the Plague).
were fain Wished or would have liked.
to be sold i.e. relinquished completely to a new incumbent.
Act of Indemnity The act passed in 1660 which granted pardons to those who had fought on the side of the Commonwealth against the King in the period 1640–60.
the Government The law.
want of temper Lack of balanced control.
pill.ruff. *Pilulae Rufi* – prescribed pills containing myrrh.

Venice treacle Another mixture which was commonly used here and earlier against the plagues.
hurries Crises.
shambles Stalls on which meat was set out for sale.
seasoning A good word – it adds something as seasoning does to food in the sense that it makes their houses smell nicer.
not at all grateful Not helpful, not appreciated.
press Recruited by force (hence the term press-gang).
they sang His praise, but they soon forgot His works A shrewd comment on human nature which, once saved, forgets the manner of the saving and only celebrates.
yet I alive! One feels the force of gratitude in the exclamation mark!

Revision questions on Sections 13–17

1 Discuss the pros and cons of the shutting up of houses during the Plague, listing carefully the advantages and disadvantages as the narrator sees them.

2 What problems faced the magistrates and examiners in trying to prevent the spread of the Plague?

3 What evidence is there, according to the narrator, that people forgot their differences during the Plague?

4 In what ways was the movement of the Plague misleading? Refer to the text in your answer.

5 Write an essay on the main elements of Defoe's style as you have observed it so far.

6 What account does the author give of the trade of the country during this period?

7 Give instances of the effects on individuals of the rumours that the Plague had abated.

8 Indicate clearly what the author believed was responsible for the lessening of the plague, and give examples of people's responses to it.

Defoe's art in *A Journal of the Plague Year*
The narrator

The mode of supposedly autobiographical narration was to become very popular in the 19th century – witness *Jane Eyre* and *David Copperfield* – but Defoe uses it to great effect here and, of course, in two other major narratives, *Moll Flanders* and *Robinson Crusoe*. The teller of the tale is the author, but the teller is also a character in the fiction. The use of a first-person narrator lends a kind of truth to what is recorded. The reader enters a real world through the intimacy which the narrator has established. The 'I' is a kind of bond between author and reader, and the bachelor saddler with his family of servants becomes a known person. If we take the opening paragraphs, we note that the tone set is that of historical truth – how the plague came about, the beginnings, the documentary records, the reaction of the people in the parishes thus early affected. The tone is assured, easy, deliberate, the narrator calling up facts, as he does throughout, to support what he says.

But as the account progresses, we come to respect his probing mind and his naturally inquisitive and resilient nature. He indicts the 'knavery and collusion' (p.27) which minimizes the number who really died of the plague in St Giles's parish. He has not only an eye for the detailed but also one for the general effects: thus he can refer to his own case and at the same time, or almost in the same breath, observe the general panic which ensued at the onset of the plague. There is a direct and honest account of what he is, how he desires to keep his business going, and of how he is tempted to leave because of pressure from his brother. The use of the word 'family' in definition of his servants has already been noted. I repeat it here because it underlines the warmth and concern of the man, which some critics have tended to ignore or play down. It also shows his sense of responsibility, though this too is put under pressure when his servant deceives him. Perhaps most humanizing of all at this time is his putting off decision, his uncertainty, tellingly mirroring our own in times of crisis. First and foremost we must remember that H.F. is a religious man, believing strongly in Providence and a course of duty. He believes that if he flees the plague he will be running from God, and though his inward debate causes him much anguish there is no doubt that he will stay. It is a tribute to Defoe's narrative skill, and particularly the maintenance of tension, that although we know that he will stay (if he goes, there will be no book) the inward debate is still full of emotional and rational doubt, so much so that he has to go away from his brother and work things out for himself.

The religious emphasis – strangely, H.F. later reveals that he is of the established church, and is not a dissenter – is shown by his turning up the Psalm 91, reading the words carefully, and then giving those words a personal application to himself. Despite his rational approach on other occasions, he shows himself here to be superstitious in his acceptance of Divine directive. From then on, though always with qualifications, he feels himself under the direction and protection of God, his faith ensuring that he will stay and also that he will take risks. The immediate human reaction, psychosomatic at that, is that he finds himself unwell the next day, though not suffering from the plague.

His personal debate settled, the narrator can now turn his attention to the events that he claims to have witnessed. The historical account reveals his personal biases. We note his puritanical streak, and his brief irony about the removal of the court to Oxford 'where it pleased God to preserve them' (p.37). He employs a graphic narrative style to describe to the reader the sights of the now infected city. We get the feeling that he loves story and anecdote, even if he can't accept the exact truth of what he has heard. And this leads us to some important aspects of his character. He is cautious in terms of rumour, preferring to deal with the facts that he knows. At the same time, because of his questioning mind, he suspects that the authorities do not reveal everything – largely in the interests of maintaining public morale – and thus suspects that the deaths listed as arising from other causes are in fact down to the plague. Although he says in these early stages that 'Business led me out sometimes to the other end of the town' (p.38) we get the impression that natural curiosity is at the root of his staying. He has an intense interest in people and events, though not in a *personal* sense, and this interest shines through the narrative. He has an historical perspective allied to his puritanism (note how he disapproves of the post-Restoration excesses). Always he manages to convey the authentic contemporary feeling, from the appearance of the comet to the appearance of the miscellaneous quacks. His account of the mass hysteria shows the narrator to be both observer and outsider – he will not admit to seeing what the woman in the street sees. He is at once a sceptic and a man of integrity. But although he disapproves of the quacks, there is an unconcealed delight in his description of their practices, advertisements etc. Defoe we know was greatly interested in the occult. That interest is widespread and still commonplace – witness the present interest in astronomy and star-signs – and H.F. is human enough to respond on a sensational level though his head rejects what he sees and hears. Again he uses these things as evidence of the authenticity of what he says, referring to the 'memorandums of these things' (p.53).

The other impression we get of H.F. is that he possesses a degree of judgment, particularly when it comes to looking closely at human nature. There is a generous tribute, repeated several times through the narrative, to the actions taken by the Lord Mayor and the magistrates, but this is accompanied by what I would call the essentially practical nature of the narrator. Consider his attitude towards the shutting up of houses, for example, where he weighs the pros and cons very carefully, considering the reactions of the people and the natural tendency to escape which so many of them show. The overall effect is not merely that of a recorder – though we are saturated with orders at one stage – but of an intensely human observer concerned about crisis, and almost planning ahead for the next one. Certainly he is obsessive, and the mention made of the fire is perhaps another underlining of his Providence theme.

I have mentioned the narrator's love of graphic narrative. The incidents with which the novel is packed demonstrate this, but we are often aware that the moral/religious content of the story is uppermost in the storyteller's mind. The Three Men of Wapping Tale is a good case in point, telling us almost as much of the narrator as it does of the situation. It shows the author's moral and social concern, and the narrator's concerns too. If we consider the way in which the three men are presented, we note that the level of rational discussion and practicality is high, that John's role is an idealized one, that the debate with the constable is essentially reasonable and that for the most part humane decisions are arrived at. It seems likely that this account represents the author's (or rather, narrator's) own idealism, what he *wants* to believe about human nature. It acts as a counter-balance to some of the violence, deception, madness and hallucinatory manifestations which have been recorded. Admittedly, in the structure of the story, the narrator needs to get outside London in order to convey the spread of the disease. But the sequence is lacking in the intense and felt realism which marks the city descriptions. It is a fable which reflects the narrator's faith.

That faith is seen in his presentation of those clerics and doctors who stayed, though always we are aware that he believes in God's will and the predominance of fate. His style is imbued with generalized compassion – he refers to 'the long course of that dismal year' (p.71). He also defines his own narrative method – almost admitting the fiction within the fact – when he says of his stories that they 'are very certain to be true, or very near the truth; that is to say, true in the general' (p.71). His perspective on the goodness or otherwise of human nature runs throughout, and he is emphatically critical of the irresponsible way the poor infected each other, or the way people moved about freely, or escaped from houses, and thus gave the plague to others.

Although it would be true to say that the narrator is actuated by general care, concern to record and an inherent inquisitiveness, the fact is that he appears to the reader, without embellishment and certainly without any self-complacency, brave. He goes into the infected areas, and we recall his visit to the burial pit and, afterwards, his going to the tavern to find the afflicted man. During the course of this visit he stands up to the revellers because he objects to their irresponsible and blasphemous attitude. The pit exercises a fascination on him, and he returns again to it in September, though still saying that he is not placing himself in any apparent danger. Defoe, through his narrator, is the natural newspaper reporter – where the sensation, where the story is, that is where he will be. We note that he is adept at making the necessary contacts in order to get as close as he can to what is happening. Here it is the sexton who gets him into the area. He turns aside from the man's story to comment on the stories about the robbing of the dead bodies. We are aware that he reserves his judgment and is charitably concerned for those who are so accused – 'I cannot easily credit anything so vile among Christians' (p.81).

H.F.'s attitude towards the tavern is a puritanical one. Yet although he is subjected to raillery by the revellers, he keeps his temper and reprimands them for their sin against God in measured language. The rational control of the narrator is always in evidence. But when he learns that the men reap the whirlwind of dying from the plague he considers, soberly and without complacency, that God's will has been done. He feels that this 'dismal time' is 'a particular season of Divine vengeance' (p.86). Despite this, the narrator displays a genuine humility. He says that he did his duty, 'namely, to pray for those who despitefully used me, but I fully tried my own heart, to my full satisfaction, that it was not filled with any spirit of resentment as they had offended me in particular' (p.87).

Another trait in the narrator is the capacity to confess error. Thus, having realized that much infection was spread by servants having to go out to make purchases, he acknowledges his own shortcomings in this respect. There is moreover a natural human reaction in his fears and his repenting of his rashness in electing to stay. The craving for experience is temporarily in abeyance. He does not wish to go out and he leads the reader to believe that he spent much time in meditation and prayer. Even these references are given with due modesty – 'I also wrote other meditations upon divine subjects, such as occurred to me at that time and were profitable to myself, but not fit for any other view, and therefore I say no more of that' (p.94) He freely acknowledges the comfort and support he received from Dr Heath (it is important that he is a good Christian as well as a good physician). This advice turns him into a practical man, who brews and bakes and conserves supplies, thus necessitating less going out and consequently less risk. Having taken all these precautions he admits 'I could not prevail upon my unsatisfied curiosity to stay within entirely myself' (p.98), though he admits that when he does venture out he comes home afraid. Not only is he afraid, he is also greatly moved both by what he sees and by what he hears. His is a sensitive nature which never becomes inured to the contemplation of human suffering. He hears stories of wicked murders, particularly those by suffocation, but he is always charitable or cautious enough to think that these may not have occurred. His sceptical nature is seen in the fact that he records that the worst cases reported always occurred at the other end of the town, so that they could not be verified. His tolerance is exemplified in the meeting with the women who are taking the hats which have been left. It is a remarkable incident, even having some humour in it which is only half appreciated by the narrator. But what he does say is significant and shows a deep well of charity in his nature – 'At length I considered that this was not a time to be cruel and rigorous' (p.105). With characteristic honesty (and not a little self-interest) he adds 'and besides that, it would necessarily oblige me to go much about, to have several people come to me, and I go to several whose circumstances of health I knew nothing of.' This sequence is followed by the story of the piper in which the narrator sets much store by truth and will not embellish the story, although he has obviously heard what he considers distorted variants of it.

Behind H.F. the saddler is Daniel Defoe the tradesman and commercial speculator. He comments on the loss of trade, and his listing of the various groups that suffered shows both his general compassion and his practical concern. He considers the plight of all those thrown out of employment, but is full of praise for the fact that they were helped by charitable efforts, and plays down any mob activity that might otherwise have been widespread. There are times when the narrator, despite all his human interest, is very much on the side of the establishment: by this I do not mean the court, but the practical administrators of the city of London, from the Lord Mayor down through his magistrates. He refers time and time again to their prudence and their vigilance.

The narrator has little sense of humour. Admittedly, the plague year would hardly call any such sense forth, but even the account of Solomon Eagle, 'an enthusiast' who 'went about denouncing of judgment upon the city in a frightful manner, sometimes quite naked, and with a pan of burning charcoal on his head' only elicits the observation 'What he said, or pretended, indeed I could not learn.' (p. 119)

His natural curiosity draws him gradually further afield, and it also takes him away from what he knows is the main sphere of infection. His meeting with the man who provisions his family but keeps away from them shows how susceptible the narrator is to the demands made on him, even if they are unconscious demands. He is moved by the man's faith and by his separation from his wife and children: he puts his pocket where his heart is, his money follows his tears, for H.F. is nothing if not susceptible. He is moved by what he sees, and returns home after this particular jaunt happy to have seen that many have escaped the infection.

His general observations of human nature find him somewhat appalled by the attitude of those people in areas where the plague had not yet reached. There is a sternness in the narrator which makes him feel that there is a need for responsibility and awareness, for planning ahead and concern for fellow beings. This is not displayed by the inhabitants of Wapping, Ratcliff and Limehouse for example. He deplores this inherent selfishness, but when he hears of extreme cases, such as mothers killing their children, he treats them with the same caution and doubt as he does all rumours. At the same time, his particular sympathy, seen in some of the stories, is given to women who are pregnant, infected, or whose children infect them or die. One gets the impression that when he says that he can only summarize certain incidents, he does so because he is himself very moved by what he has heard.

I have already referred to the story of the three men of Wapping, but perhaps one should add here that there is nothing better that the narrator likes than a discussion – even down to the practicalities between the three men before they set off. And there is one emphasis of John's which, I think, shows the narrator's character and strength of will. Admittedly, the words are from John, as we have noted, but they are important as reflecting the narrator's belief. 'Look you, Tom, the whole kingdom is my native country as well as this town . . . I was born in England, and have a right to live in it if I can.' (p.139) The essential practicalities are told by the saddler-narrator with an appreciative delight. The do-it-yourself theme which the men practise is an echo of the tell-it-yourself method adopted by the teller for his tale.

There is good reason for the narrator's continuing debate over the shutting up of houses. This is seen in his unhappiness when he is appointed as an examiner. Once more we are aware that he freely admits to natural human weakness. It is with relief that he tells us that he gave someone else some money to take over his office 'and so, instead of serving the two months, which was directed, I was not above three weeks in it' (p.182). This makes him less than good, and there is evidence too that in speaking his mind about the shutting up of houses he has not perhaps had his heart in what was required of him. Afterwards, keeping to his house, he appears to be greatly afflicted by the sights of madness which he saw when the plague was at its height. He reiterates from time to time his theme of Christian reconciliation, pointing out that it has occurred during the plague and that we should practise it always and not just in adversity.

One of his own most moving personal admissions is the statement that 'I was sometimes at the end of all my resolutions, and that I had not the courage that I had at the beginning.' (p.189) He remains in his house for a long period, depressed, unequal to the terrible things that he can see outside, yet always he recurs to God and his influence: 'I esteem my own deliverance to be one next to miraculous, and do record it with thankfulness.' (p.205) Beneath this there is the practical commonsense of the born survivor, though H.F. did not take his own advice that *'the best physic against the plague is to run away from it.'* (p.209) One gets the impression that he is impatient of people who thoughtlessly and irresponsibly spread the plague, and he notes the hysteria of the premature return. He is generous to and praises those who stayed, but he deplores the hatred and enmity set up against those who went, thinking that charity and kindness should always be shown to those who suffer. He rests finally on the assurance that God was pleased 'by His immediate hand to disarm this enemy' (p.254). H.F.'s 'coarse but sincere stanza' (p.256) shows his humility and his faith, qualities evident through his narrative.

Incidents

Defoe's method in *A Journal* is to have his supposed narrator describe a number of incidents which reflect the sufferings occasioned by the plague, and which therefore symbolize its intensity. I have given these a main heading because it does not seem to me that they are covered by the word 'Style'. They are, more accurately, evidences of Defoe's dramatic and graphic narrative art. In the simulated authenticity they balance the facts and figures which the narrator provides, conveying the eye-witness flavour which is so characteristic of *A Journal*. In a sense, the whole story is a series of incidents and, despite the fact that many of them are hearsay, the visual actuality with which they are conveyed matches the general actuality of London and the plague, the main concern of the author.

Consider the first incident, the man who sees, or rather thinks he sees, the ghost walking on the gravestone (p.44). The vividness of the experience, the unexpectedness of it in the London street, the dialogue and the reactions of the people ('he gave the people the vapours in abundance, and sent them away trembling and frighted' – p.45) all show the observation and the immediacy of the writer. The incident symbolizes the fears of the people, and also indicates the psychological effect which the plague has – here hallucinatory, later more serious distraction to the point of madness. Incidents of this kind demonstrate the outsider quality of the narrator, since he is too rational to be a party to this kind of deception (or self-deception). Another vivid instance early in the narrative occurs when the poor woman goes to the quack and by sheer persistence manages to make him 'give her his box of physic for nothing, which perhaps, too, was good for nothing when she had it.' (p.52) Consider the account of the woman left to die on her own, the master of the house and his family having fled. Here the narrative tension before the actual discovery is sustained by the build-up – the ladder, the looking in at the window, the breaking open of the house, the constable present so that there should be no plundering; all this shows that aspect of Defoe's art which rests on the cumulative effect of detail. Two incidents perhaps stand out – that of the poor man at the burial pit who is later taken to the tavern (and abused by the revellers) and the other of the piper and his falling asleep in the dead-cart.

But I suggest that the meeting and exchange with the man who ferries supplies to his infected family, as well as the parley between

John and the constable, and the mother running distracted after the discovery of the tokens on her daughter, each in its way contributes to the different effects of *A Journal*. In the structure, there is the general/historical, the factual, and the incident/story, the major example of the latter being the tale of the three men from Wapping, which ultimately becomes a series of incidents or experiences symbolic of the plague outside London. This particularity in Defoe is, as I have said, telling in its cumulative effects, for his imaginative associations with the period are given a life force through the selective incidents which animate his text.

Style

Defoe's style is, for the most part, admirably forthright, straightforward, free from images or embellishments, intent on informing the reader of facts and maintaining narrative interest by the incidents already referred to. The opening of the novel provides a good example – 'It was about the beginning of September, 1664, that I, among the rest of my neighbours, heard in ordinary discourse that the plague was returned again in Holland.' (p.23) This matter-of-fact reportage, with historical actuality, is the hall-mark of Defoe's style, which is often referred to as journalistic. It is journalistic in the best sense – accurate, judicious, interesting, carrying forward narrative or pausing to distribute facts. In *A Journal* the provision of facts is essential, since it is part of Defoe's consummate con-trick that he should make his readers think that what they are reading is the authentic eye-witness account. There is throughout an admirable simplicity and clarity in Defoe's expression, whether he is describing – the visual quality has already been noted – or reporting, or giving the reader his own particular inward debate or situation, or even the benefit of his religious rhetoric. He tabulates with the natural ease of a person who is unmindful of the fact that he is writing literature, being here only concerned with fact.

I have mentioned his forthrightness, and this is well in evidence when he contests the actual figures from plague deaths, calling the totals 'all knavery and collusion' (p.27). Such expressions of opinion are rare. Often there is the more intimate tone to the reader ('I now began to consider seriously with myself concerning my own case', p.29). Biblical references are often the reinforcement of his own religious views, or even a reinforcement of God's will, as when he quotes the prophet Jeremiah: 'At what instant I shall speak concerning a nation, and concerning a kingdom, to pluck up, and to pull down, and to destroy it; if that nation against whom I have pronounced turn from their evil, I will repent of the evil that I thought to do unto them.' (p.205)

The incidence of historical references in Defoe's narrative has already been hinted at, and these include mention of society after the Restoration (1660), the civil war, the Dutch war, and references to the Act of Uniformity and, most important of all, the Great Fire of London which is to bring an equivalent devastation in the year after the Plague. Again the emphasis on its being a visitation of God is a running stylistic presence.

Defoe is a superbly descriptive writer. As well as the particularity referred to in the incidents, there is the graphic art of the generalized account:

> London might well be said to be all in tears; the mourners did not go about the streets indeed, for nobody put on black or made a formal dress of mourning for their nearest friends; but the voice of mourners was truly heard in the streets ... Tears and lamentations were seen almost in every house, especially in the first part of the visitation; for towards the latter end men's hearts were hardened, and death was so always before their eyes, that they did not so much concern themselves for the loss of their friends, expecting that themselves should be summoned the next hour. (pp.37–8)

This speaks for itself in terms of impact and the economy which registers the passages of time and the changes adhering to it. In fact, though there are times when the narrator gives the impression of being prolix and certainly repetitious, the instances of economy in style are most marked. Look at this for an effectively concise historical summary: 'the wars being over, the armies disbanded, and the royal family and the monarchy being restored' (p.39).

His repudiation of the theatre and by implication of the Court leads to the occasional brief and ironic observation, but Defoe uses language which is manifestly not of the theatre. Take, for instance, his dialogue, which rarely if ever rings true. It is a strange comment on the undramatic language of the 17th century that the words used by the men of Wapping and their interlocutors are not true to life or, more particularly, true to the society of the time. If the Restoration stage establishes a language which is based on society wit, repartee and sexual innuendo, Defoe's restoration prose (as it affects to be, though it is of course much later) is not based on the colloquial realism of everyday speech. It symbolizes a variety of things – suffering, hallucination, prayer, debate, rhetoric – but it is a language lacking in individual drama when it is spoken aloud. We might remember here that Defoe is writing after John Bunyan, whose *The Pilgrim's Progress* (1678) also contains much idealized dialogue which seeks to elevate nonconformist purity. In many ways, it must be remarked, H.F.'s account and his experiences are a pilgrim's progress through the plague. The dissenter's style, with its biblical cadences and rational antitheses, does not make for realism.

But if the dialogue is not realistic, then it must be asserted that much of the description and the narration of experiences is. Defoe is a great lover of facts, the 'memorandums' which he claims to have written down during the course of the plague. His style shows evidence of a thorough research of sources and, if Dr Heath is Dr Hodges, of noting too the statements, advice, prescriptions of the time. Although he is well apart from his great contemporary, Alexander Pope, he has the ability to echo that master of antithesis in such phrases as 'But it was a public good that justified the private mischief.' (p.67) Sparing in imagery, Defoe can yet use the telling analogy, as when he says of the plague that 'it came upon them like an armed man when it did come' (p.136). This kind of language, albeit brief, is not a feature of Defoe's style, which is exact, close to experience, searching for the right word to express the narrator's curiosity in his record of that experience.

The use of the authorial or narrative 'I' is very common in *A Journal*. Not only does it establish a relationship with the reader, it also acts as authentication and cross-reference during the course of the narrative. We could turn to almost any page of the book and find 'I' as the variety of experience, mood, attitude: 'I was not conversant in many particular families where these things happened' . . . if I may speak my opinion, I do believe that many hundreds of poor helpless infants perished in this manner . . . I could tell here dismal stories of living infants being found sucking the breasts of their mothers, or nurses, after they have been dead of the Plague . . . I have heard also of some who, on the death of their relations, have grown stupid with the insupportable sorrow . . . I cannot undertake to give other than a summary for such passages as these . . .' (pp.133–5). I have given this at length because the 'I' is insistent and unremitting in its informative, descriptive and providential capacity.

Yet despite all this the biblical cadences, reinforced by analogies and references, form the staple of Defoe's style. The King James Bible of 1611 is undoubtedly an influence, and echoes are found in his discursive and descriptive prose. But he has a natural ease of expression, there is no straining after effect, and the result is that there is a smoothness of narration. This in fact reinforces the individuality of the narrator, even if that narrator comes alive rather through his language than his personal relations, just as *The Journal* records the character of a people (the Londoners) rather than individual characters. The language is the character, and the character partakes of much of the author. The style, like the author, reflects the time, and if the plague moves with deadly effect through the city and its environs, Defoe's fictional account moves directly and inexorably in conclusive evaluation.

Religion

The narrator of *A Journal* is a religious man who regards the plague as a visitation of God and his own survival as a deliverance. He has a battle with his conscience – and his brother – as to whether he should quit London or stay and take his chance. He has recourse to prayer, the Bible, opens his text at Psalm 91, and then determines to stay. This manifestation of Divine influence is several times recurred to, nowhere more tellingly than on the last page of the novel, where the narrator's own thanks are given wider currency by the instances he gives of men thanking God in the streets for being saved. He notes that the men were strangers to each other, but says that 'such salutations as these were frequent in the street every day; and in spite of a loose behaviour, the very common people went along the streets giving God thanks for their deliverance.' (p.255) And just before that the narrator has given an unequivocal assertion of his own belief which brooks no argument – 'Nothing but the immediate finger of God, nothing but omnipotent power, could have done it. The contagion despised all medicine; death raged in every corner . . . In that very moment when we might very well say, "Vain was the help of man", – I say, in that very moment it pleased God, with a most agreeable surprise, to cause the fury of it to abate, even of itself . . .' (pp.252–3).

Running parallel with this is the belief in predestination, often referred to in the text and occasioning a debate with H.F.'s brother, who laughingly rejects the notion, his views conveying the idea of free will, or rational decision determining what actually happens. But chance – or fate – or predestination, does play a part in the action of the novel. After he has been assured by the guiding passage of Psalm 91 that he is doing the right thing he becomes ill. At first he fears that it is the plague but, after the infection has cleared up, he is able to follow his business, and this leads him to believe that he was right to stay and that this is another sign from God. He notes the cosmic manifestations like the comet, and displays the rationality of the period both here and with regard to the quacks and charlatans, fortune-tellers and others who would debase the Divine currency. Though his own faith is assured, he deplores enthusiasm such as that displayed by Solomon Eagle or any of those people who suffer from hallucinations which he cannot share. He makes pronouncements about religious divisions, and how Dissenters were able to enter the pulpit and preach to those in need of religious comfort when the clerics of the established church had left.

But Defoe is looking back from the 1720s with hindsight, and the *Journal* shows him able to wear a particular religious hat which he never wore in life — that of a member of the Anglican church. He abhors blasphemy (hence the reasoning with and condemnation of the revellers), and he preaches reconciliation and forgiveness after the abatement of the plague, wishing that the crisis which brought sects together could persuade them to continue to practise Christian behaviour together. He notes that the actions against the Dissenters continued after their return, and we get the feeling that the broad tolerance he has himself displayed towards error, the rational basis on which he feels men should act with moral responsibility, forms the basis for his own Christian action. We remember him relieving the man who has to bring supplies for his family, we remember his going to the tavern to assist the man whose family have just been flung into the burial pit, and we remember too the three men of Wapping. They constantly thank God for their preservation and for his guidance, and there is in their moral story a kind of running Christianity — they help the party who come to the Barn (themselves responsible people who run their own prayer-meeting); they act rationally and unselfishly, practise practical Christianity, do unto others as they would be done by; form themselves into a do-it-yourself community; care for each other. We feel that the code throughout the story is a Christian code which is dismissive of differences and, although it rests on Divine manifestation, also fosters the idea of brotherly love, help for those who are poor and weak, and moral responsibility towards one's fellow creatures.

General questions

1 What impressions do you get of the narrator from a reading of *A Journal of the Plague Year*?

Guideline notes

(a) the narrator – his situation – profession – doubts – influence of his brother – debate within himself – opening of Bible at Psalms – reaction and determination.
(b) Illness – recovery – general curiosity – likes to provide facts – eye for incidents – compassion – respect for authority – organized manner of doing things – but capable of admitting error (failure to stock up etc.).
(c) instances of practical compassion – sense of adventure (linked to curiosity) – courage (going out despite fears) – confronts men in tavern – eyes and ears always alert to experience – belief in Providence (faith in God) throughout.
(d) Involved – thinks of servants as family – concerned – quick to condemn fakes of all kinds – moved by what happens – general tolerance – will not just accept rumours – balanced and rational for the most part – draws Christian morality from the whole experience – displays throughout a general knowledge of human nature.

2 Explain the various means by which Defoe seeks to convince his reader that *A Journal* is an authentic account of the Plague.
3 Write in some detail about any *three* incidents in the novel and say how they fit into the pattern of narration.
4 How would you define and describe Defoe's style? You should quote from the text in support of what you say.
5 When Defoe calls his story of the three men of Wapping a moral tale, what do you think he means?
6 Give some account of the narrator's attitude towards (a) the poor and (b) those in authority.
7 Give evidence to support your view that the narrator is a very religious man.
8 What does *A Journal of the Plague Year* tell us about human nature? You should refer to specific incidents in your answer.
9 What picture do you get of London life at the time of the Plague?

General questions

10 Write about any aspect or aspects of *A Journal* which interest you and which are not referred to in the questions above.

11 Write an account of the various quacks and charlatans, indicating some of the things that they did.

12 Do any characters stand out (apart from that of the narrator) in *A Journal of the Plague Year*?

13 'Defoe's obsession with facts has no place in fiction.' Discuss.

14 Do you think that the narrator fears a recurrence of the plague? Give reasons for your answer.

15 'The plague is itself the greatest character in the book.' Discuss.

Further reading

Other works by Defoe, and more particularly
Robinson Crusoe
Moll Flanders
Roxana
Studies of Defoe:
Peter Earle, *The World of Daniel Defoe* (Weidenfeld and Nicholson, 1976).
Maximillian Horak: *Defoe and the Nature of Man*
James Sutherland, *Daniel Defoe* (Methuen, 1937).
Ian Watt, *The Rise of the Novel: Studies in Defoe, Richardson, and Fielding* (Penguin, 1972).
Samuel Pepys *Diary*. You may find it interesting to compare his contemporary account of the Plague with that of Defoe's.